2F

The Road to a
Free Economy

János Kornai

Harvard University
and
Hungarian Academy of Sciences

The Road to a Free Economy

*Shifting from a Socialist System:
The Example of Hungary*

W · W · NORTON & COMPANY

NEW YORK LONDON

The text of this book is composed in Times Roman
with the display set in Janson.
Composition and manufacturing by the Haddon Craftsmen, Inc.

First Edition.

ISBN 0-393-02887-9
ISBN 0-393-30691-7 (pbk)
W.W. Norton & Company, Inc., 500 Fifth Avenue, New York, N.Y. 10110
W.W. Norton & Company Ltd., 37 Great Russell Street, London WC1B 3NU

1 2 3 4 5 6 7 8 9 0

To Zsuzsa

Contents

7

Contents

Preface

THE World Institute for Development Economics Research (WIDER), working under the auspices of the United Nations University and located in Helsinki, Finland, was established in 1984. The principal purpose of the institute is to promote policy-oriented research on pressing global and development problems, as well as on problems of various countries in the context of their international environment. An obvious priority of our research agenda was an authoritative analysis of the political economy of socialist systems, as seen from the perspective of a lifelong student of the problem of the eminence of Professor Kornai. I was fortunate in being able to convince him to spend part of his time in Helsinki as a James S. McDonnell Distinguished Scholar at WIDER to write a comprehensive study on socialism, one that would require intensive work for several years. This work is still in the process of gestation, but the pressure of events in

9

Eastern Europe in the latter half of 1989 has forced a hothouse growth as an offshoot—the present book. It was necessary that the comprehensive work give way for a time to a more popular, passionate tract that could help influence policy in a decisive way.

The distinguishing feature of Professor Kornai's book is the argument for a "simultaneous" attack on a range of familiar problems in Hungary and other socialist countries that have hitherto proved notoriously resistant to piecemeal solutions: a persistent excess of macrodemand over macrosupply, a domestic monetary "overhang," inflation (open or repressed) and shortages, overvalued exchange rates, currency inconvertibility, unbalanced budgets, unprofitable public enterprises, pervasive consumer and producer subsidies, a wrong structure of relative prices, and a general misallocation of resources. The mere listing of these problems indicates that they are no less endemic in many developing countries, and this fact constitutes the wider relevance of Professor Kornai's work.

In many countries the task of stabilization and macroadjustment is closely linked to the transformation of the whole social and political structure, first of all to changes in property relations. Professor Kornai is a longtime advocate of large "packages" of reform measures instead of small doses of changes that lead to inconsistencies and contradictions. This philosophy is a logical consequence of his analysis of socialist systems and of his criticism of experiments with "market socialism." As for macrostabilization, he suggests a major surgical operation. Concerning the transformation of ownership relations, he argues for an evolutionary process, which can be accelerated by appropriate policies. Professor Kornai argues, in common with many other analysts who have been critical of conventional stabilization and adjustment programs, that if resources permit, the transitional pains of adjustment should be eased by the targeted protection of especially affected groups, such as schoolchildren and pensioners. This would, however, be subject to the constraint that price-distorting subsidies be discontinued and replaced with lump sum grants or vouchers; for example, for school books and basic rations.

While each country must rely in the first place on its own human and physical resources, external resources are also very much needed. Poland, engaged in a stabilization program similar to the one advocated here, has access to a full range of external support, made available by the International Monetary Fund, the World Bank, and other intergovernmental organizations and arrangements. Other countries in the process of transformation and macrostabilization have similar needs. The type of operation described in the present book requires far more substantial external resources than are routinely available to international financial institutions.

If acted upon with adequate external finance, Professor Kornai's recipe could well revolutionize the prospects of several developing countries in Africa and Latin America that are experiencing persistent hyperinflation and other imbalances. It would indeed create the necessary domestic conditions for socialist and developing countries to absorb productively the current account surpluses of Japan and Germany that, in a climate of détente, would no longer be needed by the United States and other countries for their military buildup.

Because of the comprehensive approach it advocates,

Preface

Professor Kornai's book should indeed be mandatory reading for policymakers in both socialist and developing countries.

Lal Jayawardena
Director, WIDER

Helsinki, February 1990

Foreword to the American Edition

THIS BOOK was originally written for a Hungarian readership. I was invited to outline my proposals for an economic policy of the next few years, to be considered by the new Parliament and new government that will be formed after the first free elections in the spring of 1990. The lecture, presented on August 25, 1989, was attended by economic experts of several opposition parties and also by a few officials and managers of state-owned firms working with the present government. Out of the lecture notes of this talk grew the manuscript of the present little book.

I am confident that the core of ideas presented here is applicable not only in Hungary, but in all other countries in transition from a socialist regime to a free economy. Nevertheless, before pointing out what is *common* in the transformation of a larger set of countries, a few words are in order about the *unique* specific features of the Hungarian situation.

The dramatic changes of 1988–89 were preceded by a long sequence of important events. One has to start with the revolution of 1956, which established, if only for a few days, a multiparty political system and expressed the political will of the people to turn toward genuine democracy. The revolution was defeated by Soviet tanks and followed by years of cruel repression. When the backbone of resistance was broken, totalitarian control gradually relaxed. Hungary became a peculiar blend of more consumer-oriented economic policies (called "Goulash communism" in the West) and belt-tightening, of more autonomy for the state-owned firms (in the spirit of "market socialism") and thousands of interventions in their affairs, of rigid central controls and free markets, and also of more permissive attitudes toward and bureaucratic restrictions on private property and private activities. The same ambiguity existed in the political sphere: while the political monopoly of the Communist party was officially maintained, there was an unpredictable mixture of tolerance and intolerance vis-à-vis opponents to the prevailing political structure and the dominant Marxist-Leninist doctrine.

This long prehistory, beginning in 1956, explains the pioneering role of Hungary in experiments first in *reforming* the existing socialist system and then, after 1988–89, in stepping over the limits of reform and starting a nonviolent revolutionary transformation of the whole political and economic system. As the subtitle of this American edition points out, we are in a period of transition that is *shifting* Eastern European countries *away* from the socialist system. When the time was ripe for these changes,

14

Hungary was in some sense better prepared than the rest of Eastern Europe. It had an influential faction within the ruling Communist party committed to the shift toward democracy and a market economy. There were certain organized political groups that could draw on the moral authority and the experience gained in their past dissident struggles; intellectuals who had proved their autonomy of thought; and also political parties with a long history going back to pre-Stalinist times. In the economy entrepreneurship and private property existed already, even if they were confined to a relatively narrow field. The transformation of Hungarian society did not have to start from scratch.

Now to the many fundamental attributes of the situation common to the rest of Eastern Europe as well. When the first draft of this book was written in Hungarian (in September 1989), Poland and Hungary were the only two countries where the political monopoly of the Communist party had been officially dismantled. Today, at the date of this writing, East Germany, Czechoslovakia, Bulgaria, and Romania have joined the same ranks, and a similar development can be witnessed in Yugoslavia. In spite of the important differences in history, culture, and present political and economic conditions, all these countries have important common properties, and they will share similar difficulties in the forthcoming years.

In all of them the public sector plays an overwhelming role, and hence the countries must overcome similar obstacles if they want to proceed with the privatization of the economy. Although there are sporadic elements of a genuine market mechanism, the institutions, the legal support, and, no less significant, the culture and ethics of a well-functioning free market are not yet developed. Prices, interest rates, and exchange rates are distorted. These countries are small open economies, i.e., economies with extensive trading relations beyond their own borders, in dire need of becoming an organic part of the world economy, and yet the composition and quality standards of production are not at all adapted to the demands of the world market. A huge bureaucracy penetrates every cell of the economy's organism. Albeit in different proportions in the various Eastern European countries, similar malaises weaken the economy: stagnation or recession of real output and consumption, open or repressed inflation, chronic shortages, and, in most cases, a huge burden of external debt service. Social tensions threaten the balance of society. In most instances workers are unhappy with the protracted sacrifices asked of them for the sake of stabilization, large strata of the population sink deeper into poverty, and at the same time technocrats, bureaucrats, and managers selected by the former regime are afraid of a "changing of the guard."

The book responds to the following question: What is the economic policy to be pursued in the coming two or three years given these circumstances? The answer is calibrated to Hungarian conditions. Were the fundamentals of this policy, or variants thereof, to be applied elsewhere, careful attention would have to be paid to the conditions in the particular country. Of course, the situation in the other small Eastern European countries is very similar to Hungary's. Yet even in these economies, it would be impossible to mechanically imitate another country's policy, and the effort to do so might turn out to be harmful.

As I write, the situation in the Soviet Union and China, the two largest socialist empires, is still very different from that of present-day Eastern Europe, but in many respects similar to the Yugoslav, Hungarian, and Polish one before the drama of 1989. I think it can be instructive to readers in the Soviet Union and China to compare their own position with that of Eastern Europe these days. It may happen that our present tells something about their future. The study of contemporary Eastern Europe may help in understanding the difference between reforming socialism and shifting away from socialism; between experiments in simulating a market by "market socialism" and the introduction of a genuine free market.

More than four decades ago Hayek wrote his classic book *The Road to Serfdom,* pointing out that the way toward tight central planning, overwhelming power of the state, and abolition of private property endangers political freedom as well. The title of the present edition is an echo of the Hayek title, and considers the first section of the road in the reverse direction. We in Eastern Europe are on the road to a free society and a free economy, and we must learn how to overcome the roadblocks in our way. This is a learning process to be mastered by all of us living in the vast area from the Elba to the Yellow Sea.

I am aware that my proposals are controversial, and may meet vehement opposition and criticism. Yet I am convinced that at least the issues discussed in the book are among the key problems to be addressed in all of these countries. My list of issues is not complete, but none can be dismissed as irrelevant. Like it or not, these are among the problems that *must* be solved in the next years. The book does not offer a miraculous, universally applicable cure for all our troubles. But its *approach* can be used in all of the countries engaged in the transformation process.

This book is written to convince the reader that the shift in property relations toward privatization (chapter 1), the package of measures needed for stabilization, liberalization, and macroadjustment (chapter 2), and the strengthening of political support for these changes (chapter 3) are inseparably intertwined. None of these tasks can be accomplished without completing the others. Arbitrarily selecting some targets while ignoring others can backfire and lead to the failure and discredit of the process of democratization and economic transformation. In that sense the various parts of the program (and the various sections of this book) add up to an organic whole and offer a *comprehensive* plan for transformation. No doubt this set of proposals, being a first attempt at such a comprehensive plan in book form, has many weaknesses. Nevertheless, it might contribute to the debate over these exciting issues just because it advocates the search for comprehensive solutions instead of arbitrary, ad hoc, partial measures.

Having clarified the use potential readers in the "East" might make of this study, a further question arises: Why should an American or any other "Western" reader be interested in the subject? The term "historic" is used in a quite casual manner these days, often to describe a minor act of Congress or even a baseball game. The one event really deserving of this name, however, is the transformation of socialist systems into democratic societies and market economies. Everybody's life will be affected. There will be more reason to hope for global peace. Although perhaps not in the near future, but certainly at a later stage, there will be less need to spend vast resources on defense, leaving more for other ends: economic growth, welfare, science and culture, aid to the poor at home and abroad.

Apart from general interest in the subject, various groups of people might have a special interest. Academic experts who study communist systems will certainly follow the changes that occur in formerly socialist regimes, now shifting to another system. All programs dealing with socialism, central planning, and comparative economic systems must include in their curriculum the study of transformation processes. But, of course, the set of people with a special interest in the subject is not restricted to academic experts. It includes politicians, government officials, members of parliaments and congresses, diplomats, officers of international organizations, and economic advisers, engaged in the formulation of international politics. It also includes journalists and others working in the mass media who report on the affairs of this part of the world and influence public opinion. And last but not least, it extends to bankers, businessmen, and exporters and importers who want to enter these new markets.

All these groups need to understand the new situation in Eastern Europe. Many of their individual members have made quite a few trips to this area already and returned with certain impressions. In some instances their understanding might be correct, in others it might only be random. The deeper and the more balanced their knowledge, the more efficient will be the impact of these various groups on Eastern European affairs.

A rather common mistake is to oversimplify and suggest that others imitate one's own example. Visitors arrive in Eastern Europe laden with ready-made recipes promising instant success. "Just do what we do at home and everything will be all right." Maybe so—but maybe not. This book repeatedly reminds the reader that we have to keep in mind the peculiar *initial conditions* of the transformation process. The point of departure is the dominance of public ownership and an almighty bureaucracy with millions of hands that reach each business unit, each family, and each individual.

These are countries where such ideals as the sovereignty of the individual, autonomy, private property and private business, political and intellectual freedom, the institutions of democracy, and the rule of law were suppressed for decades. These principles can only be reestablished and generated by a historical process. It is a process that could—and should—be speeded up, but that nevertheless will not be finished in a few weeks. We have to learn from Western experience, but selectively; carefully distinguishing examples that can be followed tomorrow from other examples where the conditions of application must be created by a long-lasting evolution, and finally rejecting certain patterns, institutions, and habits that are not applicable (or not worthy of application) at all. Artificial transplants hastily forced upon these societies will be rejected by their living organisms.

What is needed is not only a revolutionary change in institutions, but also one in *thinking*. New sets of values will replace the old ones imprinted on many generations by the old regime. Let us consider one example only. A

Western reader may feel: why does this book say such trivial things as that people have the right to earn more than others if they are more successful in business? But this truth, self-evident to an American, is not at all natural to a Pole or an East German.

At each stage of his life, starting with the child entering kindergarten and ending with the old person retiring to a home for the aged, the citizen of a socialist country was told that not business, but only work (more specifically, work done in the framework of an enterprise or organization in the public sector) was the single legitimate source of income. He was taught that some inequality was tolerable or perhaps even useful for the sake of providing material incentives to people, but that there should not be "too much" of it. He was never told about the most glaring violation of this principle, as the privileges of the elite were carefully hidden from the public. Right now, in the beginning of the new era, many people in various political groups, even within strongly anticommunist movements, are still under the spell of their former indoctrination in extreme egalitarian values. They regard profit or high income as the result of unethical practices, and speculation and profiteering as sure signs of unacceptable greed.

My goal is not only to present pragmatic proposals concerning the elimination of inflation and shortages, and the easing of the foreign debt burden, but also to show the relationship between practical policy proposals and underlying values and philosophy. Needless to say, this book does not represent a philosophy and ethical outlook shared by everyone in Eastern Europe. The title points out its central idea, which is *freedom*. It is the approach of *liberal* thought (using the term "liberal" in accordance with its European tradition). Respect for autonomy and self-determination, for the rights of the individual, is its focus. By contrast, it advocates a narrowed scope for state activities. It speaks out against the paternalistic role of the state, against treating the citizen as a helpless child to be guarded by a wise (or stupid and cruel) government. It recommends that citizens stand on their own feet, and rely on their own power and initiative. Perhaps the role of government will be reconsidered at a later stage. But right now, in the beginning of the transformation process, people are really fed up with the excesses of state intervention, with the totalitarian power of the bureaucracy. It is probably inevitable that history moves not in a straight line, but like a pendulum. Following a number of decades in which a maximal state prevailed, it is now time to take great steps in the direction of a minimal state. Perhaps later generations will be able to envisage a more moderate midway.

At this point it is appropriate to explain the notion "free economy," which appears in the title of the book. A free economy is, of course, a *market* economy, but the concept is richer and refers not only to the fact that the main coordinator of economic activities is a specific mechanism, namely the market. A free economy is one that allows unhampered entry, exit, and fair competition in the market. The notion of a free economy also implies a certain configuration of property rights and a certain institutional and political structure. The system promotes the free establishment and preservation of private property and encourages the private sector to produce the great bulk of output. It is a system that encourages individual initiative and entrepreneurship, liberates this initiative from excessive state intervention, and protects it by the rule of law. A free economy is embedded in a democratic political order, characterized by the free competition of political forces and ideas. Given my own value system, the guarantee of these liberties has a high intrinsic value and should therefore enjoy top priority in economic policy-making.

I offer no predictions concerning future developments in Eastern Europe. In most of my writings up to now, I have concentrated on exploring the properties of the existing socialist systems and elaborating explanatory theories; a positive explanatory theory is expected to have predictive power. The purpose of the present book is different. I do not try to answer the question of what the role of Parliament in Eastern Europe in the future will be, but of what its role *should be*. It may turn out that some deputies act as advocates of local or sectoral interests, that some corruption occurs, that a lack of expertise hinders the efficacy of parliamentary supervision, and so on. Nevertheless, this book advocates an increased role for a freely elected Parliament in monitoring the activity of the administration and in supervising the huge state-owned sector. My aim is in part *educational.* I wish to suggest to future deputies that they be aware of their national responsibilities, raise their considerations above narrow local interests, and not bow to pressures and threats.

If I were asked to give a prognosis, I would admit that there is a good chance of strong wage drift, of lax wage discipline, of populism and demagoguery in the trade union movement developing in the near future. But this book urges: Do not go that route! You are hurting the long-term interest of labor, which requires strict wage discipline for the sake of stabilization, fast adjustment to the demands of foreign trade, and ultimately, the acceleration of growth. This is the only safe way to start the steady increase of real consumption for all strata of society, including blue-collar workers.

The original Hungarian publication was entitled *A Passionate Pamphlet in the Cause of Economic Transition in Hungary.* It does not pretend to be a calm booklet of instruction in the manner of "How to" manuals. It is a plea to the reason but also to the emotions of the reader, describing what kinds of changes are needed in actions and in institutions, as well as in values. I am convinced that my suggestions are not unrealistic; they are *feasible,* given the present political, economic, and social conditions. But whether they succeed will depend on the will of all people involved, inside and outside of Eastern Europe, and on their persistence in overcoming the many obstacles blocking the way to a free economy.

Acknowledgments

I TAKE THIS OPPORTUNITY to express my gratitude to all individuals and institutions supporting the writing of this book. For the last several years I have been studying the political economy of socialism as part of a long-term research project. The present little book is, so to speak, a side-product of this larger project, almost forced upon me under the pressure of recent events. I am grateful to the Institute of Economics of the Hungarian Academy of Sciences, Harvard University, the Sloan Foundation, the McDonnell Foundation, and WIDER (Helsinki), of the United Nations University, for their support of my projects.

I owe thanks to all those who offered their inspiring personal comments. I would especially like to thank Zsuzsa Dániel, who gave me great help. I am very grateful to Jeffrey Sachs of Harvard, who read the first English translation of the Hungarian publication and gave many

25

valuable suggestions. I received many comments from other colleagues as well; those of Béla Balassa, Tamás Bauer, Martin Feldstein, Benjamin Friedman, János Gács, Mihály Laki, and András Nagy were especially helpful.

In fact, the present edition is not simply a translation, but rather a revised edition, inspired by the first responses to the original.

I am indebted to all those who assisted me in producing the Hungarian and English manuscripts, especially to Mária Kovács and Carla Krüger, my closest collaborators, for their generous and efficient support. I am extremely thankful to all those who participated in the work of translation: Tibor Szendei, Brian McLean, Julianna Parti, and Anna Seleny.

Finally, I express my gratitude to my American publisher, W. W. Norton, and especially to Edwin Barber, Donald S. Lamm, and Susan Gaustad for their encouragement and editorial help.

Cambridge, Massachusetts, January 1990

The Road to a
Free Economy

Introduction

THE PRESENT BOOK is not meant to be a commentary on the longer-term goals of Hungary's economic development. Instead, it seeks to focus on the topical tasks of the coming years, and deals with three major subjects: ownership, macroeconomic stabilization, and the relationship between the economy and politics. It should be stressed, however, that none of these three subjects is treated exhaustively, and that several other major problems beyond the scope of this study will not be addressed.

I do not restrict myself to presenting only new and original ideas. In the course of wide-ranging discussions over the past few years, several important points have surfaced in professional literature, party platforms, and political debates. Certain parts of my message coincide with some of these well-known viewpoints, while elsewhere I state differing views or even challenge certain tenets.[1] If the reader finds something original in the book, it will be not only in the parts, but mainly in the whole, that is, in the specific configuration of policy proposals and their connection with the underlying economic and political philosophy.

The title of the original Hungarian publication is *A Passionate Pamphlet in the Cause of Economic Transition in Hungary.* My aim in calling this book a "pamphlet" is to direct the reader's attention to the fact that I do not consider the present book a proper scientific study. The prime criterion of a scientific work is that the author's statements be verifiable. Abstract theoretical works start out from precisely worded assumptions, from which they deduce their theorems. These are demonstrable through rigorous logical reasoning. In other cases, authors analyze the facts of a specific period in the past, and from these draw gener-

[1]Quite a few arguments used in this book, either to criticize government policy, refute certain ideas, or suggest practical measures, have already been made by various authors in Hungary or abroad. However, to give due credit to the originators would require extensive further studies of the debate and a much more detailed list of references. The urgency of the matter did not leave time for such research. Instead, I refer to some books and papers that concentrate on the history of economic thought in the "reform socialist" countries. They show to what extent we all fight a common struggle, even where we disagree. The ongoing debates over the issues of the transition from socialism are summed up in a number of excellent studies. Let me just single out here E. Hankiss (1989), L. Lengyel (1989), who provides a retrospective summary of the Hungarian social science literature published over a longer period, and M. Laki (1989), who reviews the opposition parties' economic programs. J. M. Kovács (1990) presents a wider international overview of "reform economics." Of course, the rapid progress of transformation and the vibrant political life make it impossible for summaries to keep abreast of the latest developments. But these studies give detailed references to the various viewpoints and include necessary bibliographies.

alizable conclusions. Then the researcher is usually expected to acquaint the reader with a body of facts, and also to reveal the reasoning that led to a given interpretation of these facts. However, these rigorous criteria are tenable only in the sphere of pure theory, or if authors address facts pertaining to the past and present only.

By contrast, those who venture into the field of "what should be done" are bound to step out of the domain of science defined in a strict and narrow sense. A proposal concerning economic policy inevitably implies a political *position,* even if it comes from a "full-time" scientific researcher, and therefore will be a mixture of subjective and objective elements. Of course, in this book I also resort to methods customarily used in scientific research, namely those of logical reasoning and reference to facts. At the same time, however, my political and moral values, my personal disappointments, hopes, and beliefs, are clearly discernible. Instead of hiding this fact, I chose to stress it by making use of the word "passionate" in the original Hungarian title.

I do not wish to conceal the limits of my knowledge from the reader. Surely many experts are better versed in the debt-service problem Hungary faces, for example, or in topical moot points of the interparty talks. But it is my hope that someone who sees the details and the everyday economic and political problems from a distance might add color to the debate. I consider myself a theoretical researcher of socialist economies (here the stress is on the socialist system in general, of which the Hungarian economy is only part). I try to explore and theoretically analyze the properties and regularities of this system. In my earlier works I made repeated attempts to contrast the socialist system with other socioeconomic formations, primarily with modern forms of capitalism. I seek to apply this preliminary knowledge here.

A number of questions treated in this book are the subject of extensive debate. Perhaps critics will judge my thinking to be in error. Even so, I will not attempt to guard against disapproval or attack by explicating my message cautiously and in a muted manner, already half recanting at the moment of expression. I would rather accept the increased risk that goes with unambiguous, assertive, and occasionally harsh formulations, because these may promote a more thorough examination of the issues and stimulate debate.

This book is not meant to be a prognosis. Instead of tracing the alternative routes Hungary might take in the future, or considering the probabilities of each possible scenario, I outline the tasks to be done and point out paths to avoid. In chapter 3 the reader will find a summary of the political conditions on which the execution of these crucial tasks hinges.

Finally, one more preliminary comment on the *temporal occurrence and dynamics* of the changes discussed in this work is needed. Some processes are perforce gradual, while other changes will have to be introduced at a single stroke, even if this causes a rude shock. A major surgery of the latter kind is described and proposed in chapter 2. Indeed, I argue that it is imperative that such a single and drastic surgical intervention be carried out as soon as possible, naturally subject to the creation of appropriate conditions for its success.

It is crucial to accurately determine the "type" to which each point on our agenda belongs, i.e., whether it belongs to the gradual processes necessitating small steps, or whether it is part of the "package" of regulations that must be executed at one stroke. On the one hand, a series of imperative measures that require a single attack should not be dragged out. On the other hand, abrupt solutions should not be sought in cases where one can and should proceed only gradually. This difference will be stressed repeatedly.

1

Ownership

IN THE following section I concentrate primarily on the private and state sectors. I also touch upon the question of whether there is or should be a third, fourth, etc., sector.[2]

THE PRIVATE SECTOR

For the sake of clarity, it is expedient to begin by making explicit the components of the private sector. They are as follows.

[2]In writing this section I was greatly inspired by the literature on the theory of property rights in general—see, for instance, A. A. Alchian and H. Demsetz (1973), H. Demsetz (1967), E. G. Furubotn and S. Pejovich (1974)—and especially by those writings that discuss the question of property rights as regards the socialist system. Among the latter I would like to single out the classic work by L. von Mises (1920), as well as the more recent works by D. Lavoie (1985) and G. Schroeder (1988).

(a) The household as an economic unit; production and services carried out within the household to cover its own needs.

(b) Formal private enterprises, that is, enterprises operating in conformity with legal statutes. Their size varies, ranging from one-man enterprises to large-scale firms.

(c) Informal private enterprises, i.e., productive or service activities and all exchanges between private individuals that take place without special license from the authorities, or that are performed without license by private individuals for formal private or state-owned enterprises.

(d) Any kind of utilization of private wealth or private savings, ranging from the hiring out of privately owned apartments to money-lending between individuals.

These four categories overlap to some extent.

Although it is often said that Hungary as a whole is in the grip of an economic crisis, I cannot fully share this view. To be sure, grave tensions and disequilibria are manifest on the macroeconomic level, affecting all economic processes and the lives of all Hungarian citizens. The largest sector, that of the state-owned firms, operates inefficiently. There is, however, a healthy part of the economy—the private sector. Although it too is grappling with great difficulties, it remains the one sector that has *not* fallen into crisis. In point of fact, the economic situation of the country is better than what the official statistics would suggest, precisely because private production and private property have developed considerably during the past one or two decades. Indeed, the private sector is the most important "built-in stabilizer" of the economy. In my view the development of the private sector is the most important achievement of the economic reform process so far.

The vitality of the private sector is proved by the fact that it could develop at all amid alien and unfriendly circumstances. In one of his oft-quoted *One-Minute Stories*—"Budapest"—the famous Hungarian writer István Örkény describes the Hungarian capital a few days after an A-bomb blast. The city is invaded by mice. Suddenly, one can see "a piece of paper posted on the ruins of a house. It reads: 'Mrs. Varsányi undertakes the killing of mice with clients' own bacon.' " We have witnessed something similar during the past two decades here. The private sector, private initiative and private property, had almost fallen victim to a series of nationalization, collectivization, and confiscation campaigns. And yet the relaxation of certain restrictions was enough to let private activity mushroom again. Turning a blind eye toward people who disregarded the letter of the law was sufficient for all those activities normally regarded as part of the second economy to catch on.

The strongest evidence of the private sector's vitality is the *spontaneity* of its spread. The organizational framework, management, and coordination of the state sector had to be devised artificially, through central measures originating at the top. But the private sector continues to develop *by itself,* on a grass-roots basis and without central instructions. The units of the private sector need no stimulation, agitation, or directives in order to act *along the lines of the market,* as this is their natural mode of existence. Conversely, the state-owned firms require perpetual encouragement and even orders to follow the market, and still are unable to do so.

In fact, no one knows exactly the size of the private

sector in today's Hungary. While statistics abound, an accurate survey has yet to be made of this economic sphere. According to one estimate made a couple of years ago, the Hungarian population spends one-third of its total work time in activities classified as part of the private sector.[3] It is probable that this sector has gained further weight since then. In any case, we can now assert that the private sector has grown into a strong segment of the economy, and one of the key issues of this country's economic development is whether or not its further growth will be successfully promoted.

In today's Hungary all proponents of various economic theories and political currents recognize a need to develop the private sector, although many statements to this effect are fairly general, even vague. This level of generality allows the economist, politician, or party dealing with this subject to remain noncommittal. Below, I set forth six concrete requirements vital to the development of the private sector. I deliberately put an edge on my words to highlight the problems rather than blur over them, as polarized formulations might help reveal the points where the proponents of various positions agree or disagree.

One more explanatory remark is needed. Should these requirements be implemented in practice, the application of some carefully considered exceptions at certain points would be necessary, and temporary compromises would also be required. The details of these exceptions and compromises fall beyond the scope of this book. Instead of resorting to hundreds of cautionary reservations that

[3]Cf. the studies of J. Tímár (1985) and P. Belyó and B. Dexler (1985).

would take the edge off these requirements, I prefer risking the use of slightly simplified formulations.

1. *The private sector must be wholly and truly liberalized.* There is no need for hundreds of new regulations that fuss over significant modifications of the bureaucratic restrictions on the private sector, and vacillate over whether to yield at one point or to maintain curbs at the other. It would be more expedient to approach the issue from the opposite direction, by giving unambiguous and emphatic statutory force to the principle that the private sector has unrestricted scope in the economy,[4] with the exception of activities that involve extra-economic considerations (for example, a ban on fraudulent or violent acts would be fully justified). Of course, there is also a need for certain legal restrictions based on economic considerations. For example, the private sector will have to be taxed; it will also be obliged to observe the regulations of environmental protection. Since these restrictions are well known, there is no need to elaborate here. The emphasis is rather on the basic principle that as a rule, the private sector should face no prohibitive measures at all.[5]

---

[4]This book does not make a legal distinction here on whether such regulations should be laid down in the Constitution or in laws passed by Parliament. Suffice it to say that there is a need for incorporating into law a fundamental basic principle to this effect.

[5]This would mean an end to the distinction between categories (b) and (c) of the private sector. All kinds of private firms become legitimate and require no special license, except for those legally banned cases that are usually based on extra-economic considerations (for example, the trafficking of drugs or children). Certain private activities could be subject to registration or official license, when this is justified by considerations of defense, public security, or other external matters.

The law must specify those exceptions where the activity is subject to license.

The substantive content of the liberalization requirement is far from self-evident. In fact, it has quite a number of components; I list only the most important ones here.

—Freedom to establish a firm; free entry into the production sphere.

—Free prices, based on a free contract between the buyer and the seller.

—Unrestricted right to rent out privately owned assets, again on the basis of a free contract between the lessor and the lessee. Among other things, these transactions should include the free renting out of privately owned apartments or real estate, with the rental freely agreed upon between the lessor and the lessee.

—Unrestricted right to employ people in all cases when the employer belongs to the private sector (household or privately owned firm). The employer and the employee must be free to agree on wages.

—Unrestricted right to accumulate, sell, or buy any article of value (e.g., rare metal).

—Unrestricted right to accumulate, sell, or buy foreign currency through transactions within the private sector and between Hungarian and foreign citizens.

—Unrestricted right to take out and bring in domestic and foreign currencies.

—Free foreign trade activity, in which the member of the

It should also adduce weighty reasons. Consequently, all other activities become legally practicable without special license. This would mean a radical break away from the current practice, in which the starting point is just the opposite: no activity is legal without registration or license. At the very best, we can expect the authorities to tolerate unlicensed activities.

private sector has the unrestricted right to export and import.[6]

—Unrestricted right to lend money, with credit terms freely agreed upon between the creditor and the debtor.

—Freedom of financial investment in the private ventures of other individuals.

—Freedom to sell and buy, at free prices, any privately owned apartment, real estate, or other asset.

It is worth comparing these requirements with Hungary's present situation. It is beyond the scope of this book to give a point by point comparison, but even a random test is sufficient to show the hundreds of legal obstacles blocking the genuine liberalization of the private sector. The existence of the informal second economy, the "shadow economy," the gray and black market, the invisible incomes (i.e., incomes earned in the informal economy and not declared for tax purposes), and so on, is rooted in the hundreds of constraints that hamper private activity and the utilization of private property. The phenomenon of the second economy may well be seen as a special kind of "civil disobedience movement," which raises its voice against senseless legal regulations and administrative restrictions. That the state has failed to enforce much of its bureaucratic restrictions on the private sector is merely a lesser evil. In other words, the state seems to have resigned itself to a situation where these activities are considered gray rather than black. Now it is high time the whole thing was painted unambiguously, glaring white.

---

[6]The state, of course, is entitled to levy customs duties. This does not run counter to the above-named requirements. This point will be discussed later.

To avoid possible misunderstanding, it ought to be made clear that all of the above-named freedoms apply exclusively to those transactions where a member of the private sector is doing business with another member of the same sector: that is to say, contacts between buyer and seller, lessor and lessee, creditor and debtor, and so on. The linkages that connect the state or some of its institutions to the private sector will be examined later.

By way of example, let us look at *foreign exchange transactions* (I cite this issue merely to give a clear idea of the case and not because I see it as the number one priority among the requirements). I would also like to make it plain that I do not propose the immediate introduction of the following measures, without taking into consideration which other measures are also taken. The liberalization of the foreign exchange transactions of the private sector can be successful only if it is an organic part of that sector's general liberalization. This in turn assumes the implementation of the stabilization program to be treated in chapter 2. And now let us turn to our example.

Requirement No. 1 does not oblige the state bank to offer me, a Hungarian citizen, the sale of an unlimited amount of foreign currency for Hungarian forints. The question of the conditions under which the state bank must exchange Hungarian forints for foreign currency, and in what amount, should in fact be settled separately from the requirements. The "freedom requirement" referred to above means that I should be free to sell my dollars on the street, under the nose of the police, and to buy them under the same conditions. I should also be free, in good conscience, to keep as much foreign currency at home as I wish. I would like to fear only burglars, not the police or the foreign exchange authority. I should have a right to offer my dollars for purchase to the state bank, without any obligation to give an account of the source of the sum. If I do not like the exchange rate offered by the state bank, I should have the right to sell my dollars to anyone who offers a better rate—a right that would entitle me to sell my forints to a private bank in Vienna, or to any private individual there for Austrian schillings. I should also have the right to take my Hungarian forints with me to Vienna or anywhere else, and to buy as large an amount of convertible currency as I can.[7]

Transactions such as these are common even today, despite being banned by law. The police are avoided whenever possible, but should a policeman witness the trading, he normally ignores it. This ambiguous situation opens up two choices. The first is to take the word of the law seri-

---

[7]The demand for liberalizing private foreign exchange transactions usually invokes the following counterargument: there is a danger that people would seek to keep their money in hard currency rather than in forints, and they would even try to take their money out of the country and deposit it abroad.

I see this as a faulty argument, a topsy-turvy treatment of the real relationships. People would dispose of their forints only if the latter's purchasing power falters. In such a situation they would strive to maintain their wealth in a value-preserving way, i.e., by investing in real estate, art objects, precious metals, and, of course, hard currency. No administrative regulation can eliminate this drive. The only solution lies in the stabilization of the domestic currency's purchasing power. This problem will be discussed in detail in chapter 2.

The depositing of hard currency in foreign countries can well be likened to emigration: it is worth the trouble only if it is banned. If the border is wide open and people are free to cross it to and fro, then the majority will surely opt to stay. Consequently, if every Hungarian citizen is granted the right to take out or bring in his hard currency whenever he wishes, and if he is free to legally exchange his money at home on the private market in either way, then there will be no special incentive to hold the money abroad.

ously and enforce it, the second is to lift the restrictions. I propose the latter.

Let us dwell a bit longer on our example, foreign exchange transactions. How does this freedom requirement affect the convertibility of the forint? It promises the evolution of a genuine market exchange rate between the forint and convertible currencies, and all this on private markets, where each client pays out of his own pocket. The requirement here boils down to the need to clear the way for a *private exchange rate* that is neither black nor gray but bright white.[8] In other words, the forint should be made convertible on the *private market*. This rate should not be determined by bureaucrats, but instead should be based on the real market forint price of the convertible currencies. Here the rate should express the value of the schilling or the dollar for the Hungarian citizen who pays out of *his own pocket*. In this situation the value of the

---

[8]Under the proposed system, for as long as the state banking system fails to introduce the convertibility of the forint, the parallel existence of two different legal exchange rates is bound to emerge. One of these rates is the private exchange rate. It represents the real *market* rate, which is based on a voluntary agreement between the seller and buyer of the hard currency. The other rate is the official one, quoted by the state bank system. It has no market character, as the rate is dictated by one of the parties (the seller when the hard currency is sold and the buyer when it is bought) by right of its *administrative power*.

There is nothing unusual in the existence of a dual rate. After all, we already have a private rate as a result of the large-scale gray and black hard currency dealings. It would be ostrichlike behavior to ignore this fact. Moreover, we can add the fact that the dual price system is also rather widespread in today's Hungarian economy: besides the official price charged by the state sector, there is also a private price used in the formal and informal private economy. My proposal is rooted in the mere cognizance of this fact, and it supports the legalization of private prices. This legalization would promote the reduction of private prices, among them the private hard currency exchange rate, because this system would no longer involve the risk premium concomitant to illegality.

forint against the schilling would be roughly the same in Budapest and in Vienna, apart from the usual transaction costs.

Naturally, the legalization of private foreign exchange circulation does not solve the basic problems associated with the rate of exchange. A comprehensive and truly reassuring solution can only come as the result of universal convertibility guaranteed by the state banking system, together with a uniform exchange rate. I will return to this subject in chapter 2. Here I limit my remarks to this: the liberalization of foreign exchange operations is an essential part of the private sector's fundamental economic rights.

These freedom requirements should not be seen as a grandiose favor granted by the state, but as basic civic rights, which have been almost completely denied to Hungarian citizens for a long time. Although the economic freedom of the Hungarian citizen has increased along with the reform process, the permitted scope of activity is still rather tight. Instead of these limited liberties, a genuine liberalization is needed.[9]

[9]I am well aware of the fact that requirement No. 1 is not followed with full consistency in a number of capitalist countries. Quite often defenders or creators of the laws that curtailed these liberties refer to these Western or Far Eastern experiences.

In my opinion their argument is mistaken in two respects. The first is historical: the capitalist countries at issue have reached their present stage after a long historical development. By contrast, Hungary has hardly begun with the embourgeoisement process following the almost complete elimination of private enterprise. The role of the state is different at the early stage of this development from that at a much later stage.

The other consideration has to do with the evaluation of contemporary capitalism. Why should we consider the current practice of any of the developed

2. *The enforcement of private contracts must be guaranteed by law.* Any violation of a private contract should entitle the injured citizen to a court hearing, and the fulfillment of the contract should be truly enforceable. This would require a judicial apparatus of appropriate size, a sufficient number of lawyers, a modern and suitably detailed body of civil law, and so on. The operational expenses of this legal infrastructure should be covered by the private sector. That is, the private sector should pay the necessary fees to meet the costs of civil courts, with the retainer freely agreed upon between lawyer and client. On the other hand, a private action should not be so protracted as to make a party to a private contract feel from the outset that there is no use taking the contract seriously, since there is no chance of enforcing one's rights.

To the oft-repeated question of what role the state is supposed to play, one possible answer is that it should administer justice in case of conflict between contracting parties, but it should not interfere in the dealings of citizens.

The provision of incentives for private savings and in-

---

capitalist countries an example to be followed? The practice of these countries is criticized from several sides. I myself go along with those critics who find fault, among other things, with the fact that in some of the developed capitalist countries the intervention in the life of the individual and in the economic activity of private property is unnecessarily frequent. In some of the contemporary capitalist countries, the conditions of free foreign exchange transactions are granted, while elsewhere there are lesser or greater restrictions.

Those who wish to cite foreign experiences should decide first on the country whose example they want to follow. Whoever declares himself an advocate of capitalism in Hungary should bear in mind that it is impossible to refer to "capitalism" in general. Instead, he should state more precisely what combination of liberalization and bureaucratic restrictions he has in mind.

vestment constitutes the guiding principle of the next four requirements. However, the method to be applied here is not persuasion but instead the creation of circumstances that would prompt private entrepreneurs to save and invest voluntarily.

3. *The absolute security of private property should be emphatically declared.* It is not the task of the present book to clarify how this could be achieved. Certainly, guarantees should be included in laws, party programs, and statements by leading statesmen.

The retroactive cancellation of the confiscation of private property is not a number one priority in this respect. This usually cannot take place, apart from a few specific, and in fact fairly important, exceptions. One such exception could be the lands of the peasantry. As far as the future inclination to invest is concerned, the most important thing is to declare in a trustworthy manner that there will never again be another confiscation.

4. *The tax system should not restrain private investment.* The tax system will be addressed later, so here I just touch upon a few points. Those committed to the idea that private investment should increase as a share of total investment would perforce agree that private savings should also represent an ever larger part of total savings. But private savings can increase only in direct relation to the advance of personal incomes. This in turn means that people should be allowed to earn as much as they can. Private production can be increased, modernized, and raised to the level of the successful modern large firms only if a considerable accumulation of private wealth takes place.

The stance taken by many politicians and economists shows a peculiar ambiguity. On the one hand, they protest the excessive power of the state, and the high ratio of the state budget to the Gross Domestic Product. On the other hand, they also speak against the excessively high incomes of the private sector. But you cannot have it both ways. Take your choice: which one do you want to complain about?

5. *Private investment as well as the formation and growth of private capital must be promoted through credit.* In my opinion the slogan of "equal opportunity" for the two sectors is a false one. In fact, opportunities have not been equal since the nationalization of 1949, and today the various sectors are positioned on uneven launching pads. To begin with, a huge amount of capital has been accumulated in the state sector; and the bureaucratic apparatus, state-owned banking, and state firms have become intertwined. Also, it is primarily the state sector that knows what strings to pull. How can we expect equality of chances between the private sector and this vast political, social, and economic power?

The legislature should also determine, within the framework of the annual governmental plan, the size of the slice from the economy's total credit supply to be reserved for the private sector. This slice should involve a couple of basic credit quotas in each credit type. For example, the decision should make explicit the percentage of the total investment credits granted by the state bank sector that will go to the private sector in the next fiscal year. Guarantees against the considerably stronger state sector's attempts to siphon off these quotas from the private sector are essential.[10] Should this governmental motion go before Parliament, the emphasis would definitely be shifted from the level of grand rhetoric to that of tangible figures. The concrete issue to be decided will be whether 5, 25, or 50 percent or some other percentage of the investment credits should go to the private sector.

While requirement No. 5 is meant to defend the private sector's right to credit from attempts by the state sector to siphon it off, it is not meant to suggest that the credits should be distributed improvidently. To remind readers: one of the credit sources has its roots in requirement No. 1; i.e., credit is granted by one member of the private sector to another. The terms of such credits are in any case fairly tough. No one in his right mind would reach deep into his pocket and lend money to another without assurances that he will be able to recover the loan. However, state banks should also set rigorous terms. The classical tools of a credit system, i.e., the various forms of securities, collaterals, and mortgages, must be applied.

Requirement No. 4 demanded that members of the private sector be free to make as much money as they can. Let me add here that they should also risk losing their investment in case they fail to repay their debt. According to well-known patterns of credit markets, various terms might emerge. The financier of a deal might grant more credit relative to the amount of money spent from the investor's own resources, provided the debtor guarantees

[10]This is similar to the phenomenon known in the Western literature as "crowding out."

48

repayment of the credit to the extent of his total private wealth (unlimited liability). Limited liability, where guarantees do not exceed the amount of private investment, should attract a lower credit share. But regardless of specific credit terms, the threat of collapse should hang over the private entrepreneur in case of financial difficulties. In other words, the private sector should face genuine hard budget constraints. Overprotection, or attempts to "grow" the private sector as a pure specimen under a glass jar, will simply make it as weak and feeble as the featherbedded state firms.

In my opinion the use of the term "entrepreneur" should be strictly limited. No one who uses the money of the state, and who makes the state pay dear for the losses, should claim this title. Entrepreneurs are those and only those who are willing to risk personal financial loss.

6. *Social respect must be developed toward the private sector.* Stated negatively, this requirement becomes still more explicit: Instigations against the private sector must cease, be they restrained or harsh. Today, people in general have great regard for peasants working on household plots or artisans laboring in their workshops. The whispering campaign is directed not against them, but against "boutique" owners or private grocers, among others. It is high time to stop branding prosperous entrepreneurs as "sharks" or "self-seekers" out of sheer envy or populist demagoguery. This kind of primitive anticapitalist attitude goes against the grain of the market, where it is most desirable that anyone who enters a deal should buy cheap, and not at all censurable that a seller should ask for as high a price as possible. If the buyer needs the product

offered by the dealer, and if he is willing to pay the asking price, then the activity of the dealer can be considered useful to society.[11] Those who buy dear and sell cheap make bad bargains—a formula all too familiar and for which the whole nation has already paid a hefty price. Clever businessmen deserve respect rather than reprobation.

Now that we have surveyed the six requirements whose fulfillment would ensure the development of the private sector, I think it would be expedient to add a few comments to these six points.

It is debated these days whether we need identifiable "flesh and blood" entrepreneurs or impersonal joint stock companies instead. Let me comment here only on the problems of the fully private joint stock companies (the issue of stocks owned by the government or nonprofit institutions will be discussed in detail later).

In answering the question, I would place the emphasis on socioeconomic aspects rather than legal ones. A most important element of the social transformation we seek is the development of a *new middle class,* whose core would be composed of industrious, thrifty entrepreneurs who want to move upward in society. From among the proprietors of such small- and medium-size units the pioneers of economic progress and founders of large enterprises would eventually emerge as the result of the market's nat-

[11]In certain specific cases there might be exceptions to this principle. For example, during a war or a famine the bureaucratic rationing of the fundamental means of existence might become necessary in order to cover the basic needs of each stratum of the population. The present book does not consider these exceptions.

ural selection process.[12] Later these entrepreneurs can be surrounded by people who do not themselves take part in the creation of new organizations, who do not found new firms, but who willingly invest in the economy through the purchase of shares or in other ways.

The critical deficiency of socialist state property consists in the impersonalization of ownership: state property belongs to everyone and to no one. In the midst of the ongoing transformation in Hungary it is time for this contradiction to be highlighted. I would like to see people take a long chance with their own wealth. Conversely, I would like to be certain that their failures will translate into real losses for them. If an entrepreneur is able to persuade others to entrust their money to him, so be it. He should be free to involve silent partners as well; if they are judicious, they will surely make a close study of the individual to whom their money will go. Within a short period we can reckon with the emergence of a few private bureaus or intermediary institutions that would enable silent partners to trade their shares. We have every reason to expect that sooner or later these developments will lead to the emergence of genuine private stocks, authentic private joint stock companies, and a real private stock exchange.

---

[12]It is worth noting that even in the most developed capitalist countries, where industries are the most concentrated, small- and medium-size firms do not die out, but continuously reproduce themselves and even today contribute a significant portion of the GDP, confirming that their existence is essential to the market. (See D. J. Storey [1983], which reviews the proportion of small- and medium-size enterprises in a number of developed and developing capitalist countries.) Over the last decades in Hungary, it was precisely the small- and medium-size firms that were liquidated in the process of nationalization and artificial concentration.

51

All these changes will take place in the course of the organic historical development of private property. It is not advisable, and perhaps not even possible, to skip over this stage of historical development, although it can be shortened by appropriate measures. The course of events is not symmetrical here. While it is possible to liquidate the private sector by state fiat, it is impossible to develop it by similar means. Here we have to reckon with a decades-long hiatus. Entire generations were made to forget the civic principles and values so closely associated with secure private ownership, private property, and markets. This circumstance cannot be ignored. The mere imitation of the most refined legal and business forms of the leading capitalist countries is not sufficient to ensure their general application.[13] A comparable attempt has already been made by those who wanted to lead African tribes, or backward village communities in Asia, straight into communism. There is no need to give the "great leap forward" yet another try.

In current political debates the question crops up whether Hungary should adopt the market economy in its nineteenth-century or twentieth-century form. Of course, it goes without saying that we desire the latter option. But there is a considerable gap between our wishes and our current stage of development, on the one hand, and a realistic pace of change, on the other. Let us look at the actual

[13]The above remark does *not* mean that we should ignore the experience of the most developed countries. It is well worth our while to learn anything that might be applicable to our own circumstances; it would be sheer stupidity for Hungary to "rediscover" through its own suffering anything that could be taken over directly from modern capitalism.

status of the private sector in today's Hungary. Apart from a few exceptions, the standard we find resembles that of the Balkans at the turn of the century, or of today's developing countries. The difference between the equipment used by the private farmers in Hungary and in Denmark or the United States is tremendous. The private farmer in Hungary does not own trucks, tractors, or silos. It is beyond his wildest dreams to have a private telephone. Let us look at the crammed workshops of the artisans. Let us look at how the private sector works in services or trade. What we find are the ramshackle kiosks of street vendors and stores that are cramped and shabby. A considerable part of total private activity is still carried out in a semilegal way, with equipment that is incomplete and, in many cases, borrowed or usurped from the state sector. In many respects, present standards fall far behind those that characterized Hungary's private sector in the late nineteenth century.

It is not simply a matter of having government fix the date when Hungary's private sector will leave its miserable, Balkanized, underdeveloped standards behind and catch up with the late twentieth-century Western private sector. True enough, we must speed this development, primarily through meeting the requirements described above. We must also turn a portion of state property over to the private sector. But the fact remains that an impatient leap would be irrational. We must expect that for a long time to come, different generations of private sector units diverging considerably from one another as regards the modernity of their legal form, business methods, and technical endowment will live side by side. We will find among them some belonging to the past century and others that are perfectly up-to-date.

This point leads to a second comment: Step-by-step changes are characteristic of the development of the private sector. It is impossible to institute private property by cavalry attack. Embourgeoisement is a lengthy historical process,[14] which in Hungary suffered a dramatic break in 1949 and was subsequently retarded for decades. In the 1960s the process was revived in certain fields, as seen in the greater role of household plots, the widening of the scope for legal private activity, and the growth of the informal economy.[15] Today, odds are that this process of embourgeoisement will gather momentum. The more consistently our six requirements are satisfied, the faster this process will be. It is conceivable that the process will not work itself out uniformly in the various branches. It will be particularly rapid in less capital-intensive undertakings in the service sector, in domestic and foreign trade. But even in the event of an acceleration in the process, it may take many years before the private sector can provide the larger portion of production; possibly a longer period must pass before a truly developed, up-to-date, and *mature* private sector takes shape.[16]

---

[14]In this context remarkable ideas and empirical references were published by I. Szelényi (1986, 1988), which influenced my understanding of this process. See also the works of P. Juhász (1981) and I. Pető (1989), and especially the pioneering activity of F. Erdei and I. Bibó.

[15]See I. R. Gábor (1979) and I. R. Gábor and P. Galasi (1981).

[16]The tempo of the Hungarian private sector's modernization and ripening will depend to a considerable degree on how tightly the country plugs itself into the European and world capitalist blood circulation. The economic culture streaming toward us from the West, Western consumers' higher requirements of quality, and the organization and discipline of business and production undertaken jointly with Western partners can all exert a stimulating effect.

I do not want to imply that the present argument is meant to idealize the role of the private sector in general or specifically in today's Hungary. I am fully aware of how common it is to find private entrepreneurs who greedily want to make money hand over fist, even by cheating their customers or by defrauding the state. Instead of striving firmly and soberly to establish their business for the years or decades to come, they consider it their priority to make the largest profit on the shortest possible terms. This kind of entrepreneur forgoes productive investment and settles instead for conspicuous, prodigal consumerism. Such entrepreneurs also tend to be impolite toward their customers, and adopt a "Take it or leave it" attitude akin to the high-hat behavior created by the shortage economy in the state sector. Together, these abuses turn public opinion against the private sector. Thus formed, public sentiment makes no distinctions, and is unjustly hard also on the honorable, industrious, and thrifty private entrepreneurs who rely exclusively on fair means for the expansion of their businesses.

Of course, we could do with further education and with the propagation of the principles of plain dealing, thriftiness, and a long-horizon business behavior. The organizations and syndicates of the private sector should also take a strong line against ethical offenses. Legal regulations are needed; among others, the prevention of cartel arrangements aimed at the elimination of rivalry, and the banning of collusion and monopoly and unfair competition. However, I am of the opinion that all these can play but a secondary role. The crucial change can take place only upon the fulfillment of the six requirements. Long-term considerations and investments by the private sector are conditional upon a sense of security of private property. The discontinuation of the shortage economy (see pp. 171–176), the emergence of competition and rivals, and the fear of business failure—these are the very incentives that can make the private entrepreneur attentive to the customer.

The last comment concerns the introduction of foreign capital. In my view the key to foreign investment should be sought in the development of Hungary's own private sector. I for one would not count on foreign capital making considerable investments in the Hungarian economy solely on the basis of exceptional conditions offered to it. At present, a number of state decrees grant exceptionally favorable conditions to foreign capital as against the Hungarian private firms. But any foreign investor in his right mind would know that these preferences are very easy to revoke. At best, he would venture an investment whose security is guaranteed by his own government. Consequently, foreign investment is bound to become a function of the home country's governmental policies.

This might well take us somewhere, but definitely not far, as is already obvious. Moreover, this situation might also attract sharpers in search of a quick and large return, ready to clear out at a moment's notice. By contrast, the serious-minded, sober foreign investor will want to find out about the status of private enterprise in Hungary. Should each and every Hungarian citizen be free to do whatever he wants with his labor power, money, and wealth, and should he be allowed to engage in unrestricted foreign trading, then the foreign investor will have no reason to be seriously concerned. I consider it rather childish of Hungarian statesmen abroad to use persuasive words in order to attract foreign capital to Hungary. It will surely come of its own accord once it feels secure in this country and no longer has to fear a myriad of bureaucratic restrictions.[17]

THE STATE SECTOR

Provisionally, I include here all the different forms of public ownership (a subtler distinction will be provided later on). The salient distinctive criterion is negative: entities belonging to the state sector are not in private ownership. Or, as the economic theory of property rights would put it: the residual income that emerges as the difference between receipts and expenses does not pass into the pockets of natural persons, and the losses are not covered by the same natural party.

In Hungary, and also in a number of the other socialist countries, the principle of "market socialism" has become a guiding idea of the reform process. This is a rather complex doctrine,[18] so I concentrate here only on the heart of the issue. Under this principle, state firms should remain

[17]It is another question whether or not it is worthwhile to promote foreign investment interest by providing proper information and by demonstrating the advantages of investment in Hungary.

[18]The literature on the debate over "market socialism" would fill a library. I mention here only the most important works: E. Barone (1908), L. von Mises (1920), F. M. Taylor (1929), F. Hayek (1935), and O. Lange (1936–37). A classic summary of the debate is to be found in A. Bergson's study (1948). D. Lavoie (1985) compiled an outstanding survey. The pioneers of the reform ideas based on decentralization were B. Kidric (1985) in Yugoslavia, Gy. Péter (1954a and b, 1956) and J. Kornai (1959) in Hungary, W. Brus (1972) in Poland, E. Liberman (1972) in the Soviet Union, and Yefang Sun (1982) in China.

in state ownership, but by creating appropriate conditions, these firms should be made to act *as if* they were part of a market. Further on I will use—and challenge—the term "market socialism" only in this limited sense: *market socialism = state property + market coordination.*

I wish to use strong words here, without any adornment: the basic idea of market socialism simply fizzled out. Yugoslavia, Hungary, China, the Soviet Union, and Poland bear witness to its fiasco. The time has come to look this fact in the face and abandon the principle of market socialism, even though a number of people still want to continue rearguard actions for this credo. I cannot go along with them. Indeed, there is a need to note the following facts.

The market mechanism is the natural coordinator of private sector activities. This is linked to the autonomy of the decision maker under the market mechanism, and to the centrality of the notion of free contract for both the operation of the market mechanism and the safeguarding of private property. It is futile to expect that the state unit will behave as if it were privately owned and will spontaneously act as if it were a market-oriented agent. It is time to let go of this vain hope once and for all. Never, no more. There is no reason to be astonished at the fact that state ownership permanently recreates bureaucracy, since the state-owned firm is but an organic part of the bureaucratic hierarchy.

During the initial, "naive" phase of the reform process, we all cherished the hope that the mere discontinuation of plan commands would be enough to create market coordination of state-owned firms. However, this hope did not come true. Instead, as several post-1968 analyses revealed, *direct* bureaucratic regulation of the state sector was replaced by *indirect* bureaucratic regulation. State authorities found a hundred means to meddle in the life of firms.[19] If a campaign managed to do away with one form of interference, another cropped up immediately. This kind of bureaucratic coordination is as much the *spontaneous* effect and natural mode of state property's existence as market coordination is of private property. Twenty years of Hungarian experience together with the experience of all other reform-minded socialist states demonstrate that this is no longer a debating point, but simply a *fact* that must be accepted.

Later, a separate point will be devoted to the issue of how the share of the state sector could and should be reduced. It is to be hoped that after this process the firms in the state sector will provide only the lesser part of total production. It is also conceivable that once the state-owned firms become small islands in the sea of the private economy, they too will be compelled to behave almost as if they were privately owned. However, this one problem is, for the time being, very far from the reality. Today, and for a long while to come, we will have to cope with the reverse situation: the tiny isles of the private sector are surrounded by an ocean of state-owned firms. The exposition below will essentially boil down to this fact. My line of thinking is, of course, contestable, but there is no contradicting it with arguments such as "Renault of France is

[19]For analyses of the relationships between indirect economic control, economic management, and the firms, see, e.g., the works of L. Antal (1979, 1985), T. Bauer (1976), and M. Tardos (1980).

also a state-owned firm, and yet it is profit- and market-oriented."

I consider the sector of state-owned firms, under existing conditions in Hungary and taken in a sociological sense, part of the state bureaucracy. The state-owned firms belong to the sphere of "government" rather than "business." They should be treated accordingly. The state sector must not be "liberalized" unconditionally; instead, we must watch it carefully. In fact, each organization of the governmental sphere tends to spend the money of the citizen in an unbridled manner. Consequently, these strong tendencies must be blocked.

The problem has already been treated in many theoretical and empirical studies.[20] By way of example, let us take an office whose leadership places a high value on performing its duties. The leadership of this "bureau" is determined to maximize its own budget. Conversely, the legislative body, which acts as a supervisor of the bureau, is required to resist this pursuit when it comes to setting the budget of the bureau.

Let us now look at the relationship between a parliamentary democracy and any of the branches of a state administration—the army, for example. The members of the American Congress must sensibly reckon with the Pentagon's propensity to spend. The state budget was created to set limits on these demands, and it is the role of budgetary discipline to enforce these limits. True enough, Congress is subject to political pressure, and the military also wants to bring pressure to bear to increase its budget.

---

[20]W. Niskanen's work (1971) is a pioneering study on the subject.

The practice they regularly resort to is all too familiar from the way state investments are treated in a socialist economy: preliminary estimates put the cost of a new military installation or a new weapon at $1 billion, but once production is under way, it turns out that the actual expenses will be double or triple the original estimate. By then, it is already too late to scrap the whole project. This is just another argument for maintaining congressional control. There are specialized committees to supervise military spending. The opposition also keeps an eye on these expenditures. If abuses occur, there is a good chance they will be discovered.

The relation between the armed forces and the Parliament is only one example of the more general relationship between the executive (i.e., the bureaucracy) and the freely elected Parliament. The former is perforce expansive, and thus it is one of the primary obligations of the latter to check this expansion. The money spent by the bureaucracy comes from the citizens and not from its own purse. It is the task of Parliament to oversee the spending of citizens' money.

Only a year ago it would have been illusory to raise this point. Today, even as I write these words, the political and organizational conditions for the legislative supervision of the state sector have yet to be realized. Such a change requires a freely elected Parliament, with deputies who devote their energies exclusively to tasks in the House, an apparatus available to each of the M.P.s, and so on. In any case, today there is a *chance* that these conditions may come about. Therefore, the time has come to make the following proposal in all seriousness: "Let us *not* give unrestricted power to the manager of the state-owned firm!"

Precisely because I am a proponent of the liberalization of the economy, I want to be liberal with the citizen and the private firm owner who will risk his own money. Conversely, I would like to see tight control over the ways in which taxpayers' money is spent. In this respect I classify the manager of a state-owned firm among the state officers. If this manager does good work, I do not begrudge him a large salary. If he is a flop, he must be given the sack. But let us not harbor illusions; the manager of a state-owned firm is not an entrepreneur. There is no getting away from the fact that he, like the heads of other state institutions, is out to expand his spending limits as far as possible.

The manager of a state-owned firm also wants to invest more, obtain an ever greater amount of hard currency, import more machinery and equipment from hard currency markets, travel more and let his colleagues do the same; and, of course, he wants to pay more wages, since this can boost his popularity among employees and ease the tensions around him. Hitherto he was free to behave in this way, because he did not have to contend with a private owner who protected his own money from such overspending. If this manager spent beyond measure, he had a realistic chance to obtain relief: the state budget or the banking system was sure to help him out. As long as the state sector remains the dominant sector in the national economy, the firms, owing to their spontaneous and internal concerns, do not have and will never have hard budget constraints. It is time to abandon hope that the budget constraint can be hardened.

I wish neither to oversimplify nor to be extreme. I do not maintain that the state firm is simply one among many kinds of public offices, and differs in no way from, for example, the Highway Police Department or the Tax Office. Nor would I say that the state-firm manager's attitude resembles in all respects that of a mayor or a metropolitan police chief. The state firm sells its products for money, operates on the basis of revenue and cost calculations, and maintains a relationship with sellers and buyers. In this sense, characteristics of the businessman appear in the behavior of state-firm directors, and in the two decades that have elapsed since the 1968 reform, these characteristics have unquestionably been strengthened. It would be a great shame to weaken these attributes. But at the same time, all responsible directors, from the highest to the lowliest manager, must realize that each and every one of them is a state officer entrusted to dispose of state funds. In this they must be held fully accountable, and it is entirely justified that the citizens' representatives oversee their work.

Several practical suggestions follow from the foregoing. It is not the task of this book to elaborate the technical and administrative details of the suggestions; I will only outline basic principles.

1. The director of a state firm should be completely independent in the following decisions: the composition and quantity of output, the combination of inputs and choice of technology, agreements with the suppliers of inputs and with the purchasers of outputs, and the hiring and firing of labor.

Nominally, these decisions have been in the firm's independent sphere of authority, but in practice higher organs interfere in a hundred different ways. For my part, I favor a more complete, consistent realization of independence. As a matter of fact, I would call for a kind of independence for the state firm akin to that enjoyed by individual plants *within* very large private firms in developed capitalist systems. Typically, the manager of the subunit is free to make numerous decisions independently, while the large firms' headquarters decide on basic financial targets.[21]

2. On the whole, the determination of the selling price should belong to the state-firm directors' independent sphere of authority. The state firm (that is, the seller) determines, without official intervention, the price of products and services that in the market economy are generally set by the producer. This power is complemented by the state firm's independent authority as seller to agree freely with the buyer (state firm or private buyer) on those prices that under normal market relations would be voluntarily agreed upon by sellers and buyers.

In justified cases the authorities should continue to prescribe prices; these, however, must remain only exceptions to the general rule of free price determination. These exceptions will be addressed in chapter 2.

Now we come to those spheres of authority in which, from my point of view, it is necessary to *restrict* the independence of the state firm.

---

[21]Many studies have been published on, for example, the way the various subordinate units receive partial autonomy within the huge capitalist firms. This partial autonomy implies that the subordinate unit is treated as if it were self-accounting and producing for its own profit. Actually, this is not the case, since the genuine owner, the huge capitalist firm, stands in the background.

3. Most important: the state banking system must strictly control the granting of credit to the state sector. Tight monetary control must be enforced. We must not yield to any type of pressure in this regard.

4. We must require similar strictness of fiscal discipline in relations between the state treasury and state-owned firms. Later, in chapter 2, we will discuss the subject of ultimately ending the subsidization of loss-making state firms. Here, I only wish to say that until then, we must also set strict limits on the practice of compensating firms for losses; taxes must be collected, and in general we must put an end to bargaining between the treasury and state-owned firms.

5. The wage policies of state firms must not be liberalized. This point of view runs directly counter to the widespread opinion that the state firm should have total independence in this area as well. We will return to the justification for my suggestion, and in general to the question of wage discipline.

6. The danger remains that the unbridled state firm will spend hard currency on imports, in the hope that it will somehow be able to find the forints to cover this purchase of hard currency. I formulate my suggestion in two alternative forms:

(a) If we complete the stabilization operation described in chapter 2, if we manage to restrict with iron consistency the supply of credit to state-owned firms, and if, in addition, we attain the convertibility of the forint at a realistic rate of exchange, then and only then can we lift the special limits on state firms' purchases of hard currency. Then forints will be available on a restricted basis to the firm, and the demand for hard currency will thereby be held in check.

(b) If the conditions summarized in point (a) are not met, then the state-owned firms' purchases of foreign currency must be restricted by direct administrative means.

7. The state-owned firm should be independent in those investment decisions that it can finance from its own savings or bank credits, or through funds obtained on the capital market. If, however, the central or local state budget also contributes to the financing of investment, or if the credits are backed by state guarantees, then that legislative body (Parliament, local council) that oversees the state organization financing the project must also approve it.

Parliamentary decision is also required when the implementation of investments is tied to intergovernmental contracts. We must not present current and future generations with a *fait accompli*, as happened in the past in the case of such already notorious investment projects as, for example, the Bős-Nagymaros Danube Power Station, or the Hungarian participation in the construction of the Siberian gas pipeline in the Soviet Union. If an investment promise turns out to be a losing proposition or dangerous in any other respect, it can be called off. Naturally, since decisions of this latter kind usually involve considerable losses, it would be far more expedient to launch the investments only after due consideration. The elected representatives of the people must be granted the right to reach a responsible decision *prior* to the opening of the huge state purse or the signing of the related international contracts.

8. I mention the following point only for the sake of completeness, since it will be addressed in detail later: The

managers of the state-owned firm do not have the right to sell the enterprise. This is the right of the *owner,* whereas the manager is only a paid employee.

I do not believe that, taken together, the autonomy described in points 1 and 2, or the limits to autonomy discussed in points 3 through 8, would ensure efficient operation of state firms. Let us be clear: this is a *vain hope.* The state firm carries its own fate within itself, especially as long as the state sector predominates in the economy; there is no wonder drug that will make it operate at a high level of efficiency. It is true that inefficiency in the state sector cannot be a matter of indifference to anyone, and the above suggestions might help lessen it. They are, however, primarily justified by other goals, of which I emphasize two.

The most important is the *protection of the private sector.* The country's resources are limited; both the state and private sectors want to utilize them. But the two sectors' chances as rivals in the competition for resources are not equal. The state firms' appetite for resources is virtually insatiable, because they are accustomed to the soft budget constraint, while the hard budget constraint places a limit on the demand of the private sector. The state firms have well-developed connections with the banks and the authorities, and their large size in itself ensures many advantages for them in the procurement of resources. The tight restriction of credit extended to state enterprises, the regulation of the wages they pay out, the supervision of state investments, and other restrictions are necessary to protect the private sector from being crowded out by the state sector's tendency to siphon off resources. Those who take seriously the task of developing the private sector cannot allow for the shares of the two sectors in the resource distribution to be determined by the free play of political and economic forces.

I am not a supporter of the oft-heard slogan calling for equal terms of competition for the two sectors. I argue instead, unapologetically, that all sectors of the national economy need not be treated uniformly. Those who spend state funds cannot claim the same rights as those who have to rely on their own resources. In the latter case, the citizen who spends his own money invokes the exercise of a basic human right. In the former case, where the money comes from the state's purse, society should exercise tight control. Just as the exhortation "Hands off the private sector!" is fully justified, there is also the need to demand that the state sector be controlled with a strong hand.

This idea is squarely opposed to current practice, i.e., to the bureaucratic restriction of the private sector and to the liberalization of the state sector. My viewpoint also runs counter to that of several economists and politicians, who in their proposals and platforms repeatedly argue for the continuation, and even expansion, of present-day policies: they want to ensure unlimited liberalization for state-owned firms while maintaining hundreds of constraints on the private sector.

The second, equally important goal justifying the restriction of state-sector demand is that of *macroeconomic stabilization*. As will become clear from chapter 2, the strict enforcement of fiscal, monetary, and wage discipline is indispensable, as is careful deliberation prior to any decision concerning investments whose implementation involves the use of state resources. In the above analysis Parliament's role has been referred to repeatedly. I do not want to dwell here on what the working relationship between the future Hungarian Parliament and the bureaucracy elaborating the economic plans for the state sector of tomorrow's Hungary should look like. In shaping these contacts, we will have to consider the experiences accumulated under the monolithic structure of the planned economy in the relationship between the leading political bodies and the lower-level economic institutions (bargaining processes, distortion of information).

We will also have to weigh the pros and cons of the experiences of the developed parliamentary democracies, i.e., the working relationship between Parliament and the state bureaucracy in these countries. At the same time, we must recognize that no parliamentary democracy has ever faced such a vast state sector as the future Parliament of Hungary will have to face. If we do not want the decisions of our future Parliament to remain a rubber stamp on the motions of the bureaucracy, and if we want to avoid the crippling of the state sector by endless parliamentary debates, then we have no other choice but to try to steer cooperation between Parliament and the state sector toward a negotiable middle course that avoids both excessive intervention and unlimited liberalism. It is vital for all political forces to have their own small expert bodies, which then enable them to exercise genuine control over the state sector without ever having to needlessly interfere in its everyday activity.

In addition, we need to develop a range of institutions under parliamentary, not governmental, supervision, institutions that will provide an effective counterweight to the state administration. A start has been made. A State Audit Office patterned after those found in many parliamentary democracies is being set up to oversee spending by the state apparatus. Another new institution, designed to manage the privatization of state property, is likely to be supervised by Parliament, and it would be practical for the central bank, the National Bank of Hungary, to be under parliamentary control as well. No doubt a good many other organizations independent of the government machine will be required.

I do not want us to expect too much of the future Hungarian Parliament. A process of organic development and a long period of learning will be required before deputies and the institutions answerable to them are proficient in their tasks. That implies a very important part for the press and public opinion as a whole in monitoring the state sector, particularly during the learning period, but also later on. The business results (profits or losses) of state-owned firms must not be kept secret; those who ultimately foot the bill—the citizens of the state—must be kept informed.

It logically follows from all that has been said about the inevitable bureaucratic traits of state ownership that I myself am deeply suspicious of the brand of so-called "property reform" that assigns state property to another state-owned institution or firm in various legal forms (for instance, by transferring shares) instead of placing it in truly private hands and that is carried out with inadmissible haste in Hungary today. Similarly, I am quite suspicious of the "state capital market," which I consider to be one of the most grotesque absurdities of the whole Hungarian reform process. The past decades were replete with pseudo-reforms; what we are experiencing today is the latest wave of these fake, illusory changes. We have seen that an organization is out there with the authority to spend the money of the state, and which does so irresponsibly. The so-called solution works as follows: let us hand over the ownership rights held by this state organization to another state organization, which in turn continues to spend the money of the state irresponsibly.

The changes I am wary of are manifold. One of them the Hungarian economic lingo refers to as "cross-ownership." In this scheme one or more state-owned firms become joint owners of yet another state-owned firm. A further change is the intertwining of the state-owned commercial banks and certain other state-owned firms. The bank acquires part of the shares of the state-owned firm, or conversely the state-owned firm becomes a shareholder of the state-owned bank. Yet another form is something called "institutional ownership," a scheme in which a state-owned insurance company or a city council buys into the shares of a state-owned firm.

These forms have been introduced at least partially, and these changes in general are rapidly gaining ground. Some studies produced by Hungarian reform literature have long pushed for these changes, and there are others that still urge their further spread.[22] But however strong this

[22]I cannot offer a survey here of the entire literature on this idea, and it does not fall within the present book's province to assign priorities among them. My impression is that M. Tardos' influence was the greatest (among his most recent works, see 1988a and b). See also T. Sárközy (1989). Similar thoughts were

current may be, both on the level of ideas and intellectual debate and in actual practice, I am determined to speak out against it. I daresay that I am not the only one around who is fed up with this practice of simulation. We have already tried our hand at simulating quite a number of things. The state-owned firm simulates the behavior of the profit-maximizing firm. Bureaucratic industrial policy, regulating the expansion or contraction of various branches of production, simulates the role of competition. The Price Control Office simulates the market in price determination. The most recent additions to this list are the simulated joint stock companies, the simulated capital market, and the simulated stock exchange. Together, these developments add up to Hungary's Wall Street—all made of plastic!

The Westerner who hops over here for a couple of weeks from, say, the World Bank or the International Monetary Fund may fall under the spell of these simulations; visitors from abroad tend to be fond of experiences that seem familiar. The Westerner strolling about in Budapest will be pleased at the sight of a McDonald's, simply because it recalls the familiar taste of a Big Mac. Similarly, it is a pleasure for him to see here the familiar banks, joint stock companies, or the stock exchange. Odds are that he will not notice that these same banks, joint stock companies, and stock exchange are but fakes. What is going on here is a kind of peculiar "Monopoly" game, in which the

---

published by the Consultative Committee for Economic Management (1988). A thorough survey of the debates in Hungary on the ownership reform in the state sector is to be found in J. Bársony (1989) and L. Lengyel (1989, pp. 153–185).

gamblers are not kids but adult officials, who do not play with paper money but risk real state funds.

Whenever I get to this point during a conversation, the following counterargument is voiced: "Why don't you just take a look around today's capitalist world? There too one can find plenty of joint stock companies, the majority of whose shares are also held by other firms, insurance companies, nonprofit institutions (e.g., pension funds or universities), or local governments." Why indeed do I expect the ratio of this nonprivate form of ownership to be any smaller in Hungary than in the contemporary capitalist systems?

It is my firm conviction that history is not like a film reel that can be stopped at any moment, or run on fast forward or backward at will. Socialist state ownership means the complete, 100 percent impersonalization of property. We cannot simply reverse this process in an attempt to reduce the percentage gradually to 95, 90, 85 percent and so on. The reel must be fully rewound and played from the beginning. Let us look more closely at the past and current developments in the capitalist world. We have already touched upon this issue in the analysis of the private sector in today's Hungary. Let us pick up the thread again with a brief outline of the dynamics of the centuries-long capitalist development.

The first engines of capitalist development in all countries are individual entrepreneurs; they are the smartest and luckiest small-timers who either quickly or through successive generations accumulate capital. This is true for the history of capitalism in each country at the national level, and also for the history of most individual big capitalist firms within particular countries. Entrepreneurs enter and exit; some survive while others go under. There are those who get stuck at the level of shabby shops or modest, medium-size factories, and also those whose ventures grow into mammoth companies. In the meantime the acquisition of more impersonal capital is also going on continuously; this capital belongs to people who place their savings in bank deposits or shares. With the strengthening of the security of ownership, the development of a related legal infrastructure, and the ethical norms of fair business management gaining ground, we can expect the parallel spread of various forms of nonprivate investments. Of course, this process also implies that the state acts as the guarantor of sound business dealings.

All things considered, many of these institutional investment forms are in the last analysis backed up by an interest by ultimate private owners. This interest exercises pressure on the behavior of the nonprofit institution's investment. Or there is a fairly powerful institution—for example, a university or a foundation—in the background, which has its own traditions and its own organ of genuine self-government. Certainly this institution will use a firm hand to ensure that its investments pay off, all the more so because it is also financially autonomous and because it cannot count on the paternalistic patronage of the state. The ratio of nonprivate investments will thus grow as a function of this process.

But two qualifying comments should be added here. First, if the undertaking is truly new, then it is only rarely a nonprivate investment. Most important new products of the past fifty years were backed by identifiable enterprising

individuals or groups who financed the whole process
from their own pocket. The only major exceptions were
innovations that were closely connected to military development and large infrastructural projects. It seems natural
to expect that the central government should raise the
necessary capital for the construction of a new airfield,
and in the process cooperate with the local authorities.
But this would be an exception to the rule usually followed
when something genuinely new is being introduced. The
normal course of events is the following: the pioneers
make a sizable profit on the new product in the new industrial branch or the new market, but they are also the ones
to foot the bill when the venture strikes the rocks. The
initiator's capital is often rounded off by outside private
investors, primarily by those who are ready to take a long
shot in the hope of an exceptionally high profit.[23]

The second qualifying comment is in fact a question:
Why should the degree to which property has become im-
personalized in contemporary capitalism be a guide for
Hungary?

I am fully aware that joint stock companies play a large
role in highly developed contemporary capitalist countries, and that there is at most an indirect linkage between
the millions of shareholders in corporate business and the
control of the corporations. Using Albert Hirschman's
well-known dichotomy, the small shareholder expresses
his disappointment rather by "exit," i.e., getting rid of
shares that do not appeal to him anymore, than by

[23]In the United States and other developed industrial countries, specific financial institutions are formed to finance these kinds of "venture capital."

"voice," i.e., directly influencing the management of the firm. Many private owners do not decide on their investment portfolio directly but use the services of intermediary agencies. In a modern capitalist economy, thousands or tens of thousands of insurance companies and pension funds have sizable shareholdings in big corporations. The "little" private owner is far away from the dealing on Wall Street. His money is at stake; the profitability of corporations will ultimately affect his personal wealth and well-being, but this connection is established through long and indirect linkages, and has become impersonalized to a certain degree. Yet in spite of these well-known facts, Hungary today does not have to imitate the contemporary United States or Japan. If, for example, the proportion of institutional ownership stands at 42 percent in Japan and 37 percent in the United States (of course, these are fictitious numbers), then do we really have to follow this 37 to 42 percent pattern?

In the West the impersonalization of property is criticized as well, and in my view these criticisms are often accurate. Ironically, the germs of socialism are already present in today's capitalism. There are many who believe that ownership has become inordinately impersonal in the insurance industry, health services, and banking. In the United States we see today a classic example for the softening of the budget constraint, namely in the sphere of savings and loan associations specializing in financing housing projects. Many of these associations have already gone bankrupt, in many cases because they abused the confidence of the depositors and accorded credit en masse to contractors who proved to be unreliable debtors.

The pattern is all too familiar to a Hungarian economist. Now it is the state's turn to reach deep into its pocket and rescue these associations. If the state failed to do this, depositors would trigger a run on these units, and this in turn might result in a grave financial crisis similar to the recession of 1929. But is this really an example for us to follow? Certainly not! Many American economists believe that considerably harder constraints should have been applied in these associations right from the outset, and the conditions of state guarantees should have been made more clear-cut. A country like Hungary must take special care not to follow such a pattern, since in this country unswerving confidence in the paternalistic role of the state has formed deep roots over the past few decades.

Now let us come back briefly to the salary of the managers of the state-owned firms. I look upon the successful manager of a state-owned firm as a highly esteemed official, whose prestige is no less than that of an ambassador, a mayor, or a general. But make no mistake: he is not a businessman. If he does his job well, he should earn good money. However, his wages should not be allowed to reach astronomical figures. I disapprove of this not just because the country is now facing great difficulties. If the country were well off, a manager in the state sector would still remain an official paid out of the state budget, and not a person licensed to manage the money of private individuals. It is the task of the deputies in Parliament to fix the salaries of the prime minister and the generals; the same body should likewise set the ceiling for the wages of state-owned firms' managers.

As mentioned before, the partial decentralization that

Hungary has accomplished as part of the reform process has developed a few qualities in the managers of state-owned firms that approximate those of genuine businessmen. It is reasonable to expect that these developments will become manifest in their financial and moral incentives as well. While no one would reasonably propose that an attorney be paid a bonus in proportion to the total number of years spent in jail by convicts, it might well be justified to hold out the prospect of bonuses on top of their fixed salaries to managers in state firms. But the share of these extras should remain moderate. In the midst of the mostly arbitrary and distorted price and tax systems of today's Hungary, the economic definition of "profit" remains a major bone of contention. It is unjustified from an economic point of view to use some kind of formula to link the bonus to be paid to the manager in the state firm with the firm's so-called profit.

When I propose that Hungary's future Parliament set the upper limits on the wages of managers of state firms, I do not consider it necessary to apply similar measures to managers contracted by private firms. If the owner of a private firm wants to pay one million forints a year from his own pocket to any of his employees, he must be free to do so; he knows whether it is worth it or not. But no one has the right to draw an arbitrarily fixed amount of money in wages from the company pay desk or to have this sum approved by any administrative authority, if the money comes from the state budget.

Let me give a telling example. There is debate now about whether Hungary should undertake to host the 1995 World Expo. The issue is scheduled to go before

Parliament, where the deputies will vote on a motion by the government or one of its subsidiaries. I propose the following.

Those government officials, committee members, and ministerial commissioners who assume responsibility for the motion should offer as mortgage their own personal assets: their condominium flats, private houses, second homes, cars, or art objects. An appendix to the motion should include a full inventory of these assets. The persons involved should be free to determine which part of their private wealth they want to keep out of the mortgage charge, but it should also be clear that the assets they burden with mortgages are dear to them. Of course, the value of these assets will cover only a fraction of the expected investment costs. But these mortgages should still represent a considerable part of these persons' total material wealth accumulated during their life work.

The bill on the World Expo should hold out the prospect of a lavish bonus for the drafters of the motion, on the proviso that the event will come off as promised. The same bill should prescribe the full foreclosure of the mortgages in case the exhibition is a failure.

In my opinion these conditions would make it perfectly clear to the drafters what it is like to run a risk that might affect their own pocket. If under these circumstances they should choose to opt out of the whole proposition, they will, of course, have the right to do so.

Let there be no misunderstanding. I am not recommending that the government of any country should follow such a procedure with any piece of draft legislation. I make the suggestion half-jokingly to illustrate a serious point. Indeed, Hungarian citizens are frustrated, because it has become a matter of course over forty years for party and state functionaries to make decisions on billions of forints and gigantic projects with the stroke of a pen. If the projects bore fruit, fine; if not, too bad—the officials themselves never lost a penny. This extreme example is also intended to show that a link must be established at long last between the decision maker's own pocket and the economic decision he initiates.

SHIFT IN THE PROPORTION OF THE TWO SECTORS: THE PROCESS OF PRIVATIZATION

I consider it desirable to increase the proportion of the private sector as fast as possible to a point where this sector accounts for the larger part of the country's Gross Domestic Product. This, however, can be achieved only through an organic process of development and social change. This process is not a recent development but has been dragging on for one or two decades already. The task is now to accelerate it by implementing a number of practical measures.

I am not fond of the slogan "reprivatization." Margaret Thatcher had grounds to implement the policy behind that slogan in Britain, where the private sector had survived the period of nationalization. Moreover, in Britain there is enough domestic capital to buy up the state sector, and at fair market prices (although I must add that reprivatization is also facing difficulties there).

Now what are the aims that can reasonably be achieved in Hungary, and what are the points I consider prejudicial? Let us examine the latter first.

State property must not be squandered by distributing it to one and all merely out of kindness. This phenomenon crops up in countless forms at every turn. For example, it is absolutely unjustified to sell state-owned apartments to tenants at a price that is but a fragment of the real market price. To make matters worse, the buyer has to deposit only a trifling portion of the purchase price in cash. A former tenant can thus obtain a hundred-square-meter apartment in Buda, in the most expensive quarter of the Hungarian capital, by paying in cash no more than the equivalent of the real market price of one square meter of the apartment. This is sheer nonsense, especially in view of the fact that the same tenant had for decades been subsidized by the state through low rents.

My factual knowledge is incomplete as regards the number of stocks private individuals obtain in the course of the current drive to transform state-owned firms into joint stock companies, and I am also unacquainted with the current quotations managers and other employees of the firms are offered. A limited right of preemption and some discount seem justified to a certain extent. But it would be completely wrongheaded to let anyone become a stockholder for a song, be he a manager or just a staff member of a firm.

The proposal has been made that state wealth should be distributed among the people as a matter of civil right. This scheme would entitle each citizen to receive a whit of capital, which he or she would be free to invest or sell.

81

This proposal is mistaken. It leaves me with the impression that Daddy state has unexpectedly passed away and left us, his orphaned children, to distribute the patrimony equitably. But the state is alive and well. Its apparatus is obliged to handle the wealth it was entrusted with carefully until a new owner appears who can guarantee a safer and more efficient guardianship. The point now is not to hand out the property, but rather to place it into the hands of a really better owner. A precondition to this is that genuine private entrepreneurial motivation should gain ground and take hold.

Let us turn our attention to my positive proposals.

1. The members of the private sector should be given a chance to buy the wealth of the state sector in suitably separated parts. The household should be free to purchase state-owned realties (apartments or even apartment houses, lots, stores, and so on). Private entrepreneurs should have the right to acquire state-owned enterprises. It would obviously be unrealistic in today's Hungary to count on private entrepreneurs to purchase huge state-owned firms. But they should have opportunity to buy smaller enterprises. This could be facilitated by breaking up the enormous Hungarian enterprises that artificially unite a number of smaller units. These units could then be sold to private entrepreneurs. The principle of "double or quits" must never be applied here. It is feasible to split an artificially inflated mammoth into ten smaller and healthier units, sell, say, five of these units, and keep the rest under state management.

This process of passing state property into private hands should in no way lead to the brutal dismantling of huge, indivisible units. Today's Hungarian economy is inordinately concentrated, even as compared with the concentration rate of the developed industrial countries. There are plenty of opportunities to create smaller units, but there is no need to act overhastily either. In this context it is indispensable to thoroughly analyze the concentration structure of genuine market economies, where competition has resulted in a kind of natural selection. In those economies the large, medium, and small enterprises and even the people engaged in home industry coexist and cooperate. Hungary needs all of these plant sizes.

It would be unwise to employ uniform methods irrespective of the branch of the economy or the size of firm concerned. A different procedure must be used for a giant firm than for a state-owned grocery or a small automobile repair shop. The same applies in choosing between all the forms of privatization considered in points 2–8 below. It is comparatively simple to transfer smaller units from state ownership into the hands of an individual or group of individuals. The larger the unit involved, the more necessary other legal forms become. (See the comments on the joint stock company in point 9.)

2. Irrespective of its size, state property to be sold to a private owner should change hands at a real market price. The property should generally be auctioned, and the potential buyers should always be notified of the public sale. Because of the fact that in many instances there is no guarantee that the state institution, which acts as the nominal disposer, is really interested in fixing a realistic (suitably high) selling price, it might be useful to involve independent bodies in quoting the asking price. In certain kinds of

sales the asking price is easy to fix; on the housing market, for example, the price level of the private market offers an appropriate starting point. Of course, when it comes to the sale of producing firms, the task turns more difficult. Here one could start out from the question of how much the private entrepreneur would have to invest from his own money in order to establish a producing unit similar to the one on offer.

3. A credit construction related to the sale of state property to private owners must be established. The following example, which outlines a possible structure for such credit deals, is meant to illustrate the point and should in no way be seen as a polished proposal.

A private individual or group wants to acquire state property valued at twenty million forints (in accordance with what has been said in point 2, we suppose that this is the real price without any reduction). The potential buyer is obliged to make a down-payment of five million forints to the seller, and he will have to pay off in equal installments the remaining fifteen million forints plus interests in no more than five years. The twenty-million-forint state property at issue becomes private property at the very moment of this transaction, but it remains charged with a mortgage to the value of the debt.

This mortgage must be tough. If the new private owner fails to make his installment payment when due, he will lose a proportionate part of his original investment (following the necessary legal proceedings), and the property will revert to the state body that transacted the credit construction.

The crux of this example lies not in the numerical proportions or the organizational form (i.e., it is beside the point here to name the source of the mortgage loan or the institution destined to enforce the credit contract). My aim is rather to illustrate two important economic policy requirements. First, that the upper limit on sales to private parties is not determined by the current total of private wealth. If the private sector currently holds one hundred units of capital expendable for buying state property, then it is possible for it to purchase several hundred units' worth of state property, with the difference to be covered by way of credit. So as far as this problem is concerned, it is possible to accelerate markedly the process of transferring state property to private hands. Second, this credit should be granted to real flesh-and-blood persons instead of distributing it through an intangible stock market. This flesh-and-blood person should be entitled to a sizable credit, but once he fails in his payment, he should face the complete loss even of his initial capital.

4. The practice of leasing out state assets to private individuals is already widespread in Hungary. This practice is definitely needed. However, there are two kinds of mistakes to be avoided. One of them occurs when the state-owned firm, acting as the lessor, is greedy and demands an irrationally high rental. This can only incite the lessee to ruthlessly exploit the property of the state; he will squeeze out everything he can from it, then move on. The other mistake is when the lessor squanders state property by setting a gratuitously low rental. In short, rentals must be rational and realistic.

The rental system can also serve the transition to sales. On the one hand, the lessee can gain experience and the ability to decide whether it is worth buying the state asset at issue. On the other hand, the state owner can discover a realistic asking price. There are well-known formulas for converting rents into nonrecurrent capital value.

5. Part of Hungary's state wealth can be sold to foreign owners, but only to the extent compatible with the nation's interest. No economic hardship can justify the bargain-basement sale of national wealth.

Let us consider the interests of foreign capital: it comes to Hungary not out of kindness but mainly to make a profit. Other motivations may also play a role. For example, foreign capital might regard Hungary as a beachhead and initial training ground in capturing the Eastern European market. In any event it is understandably guided by its own interests, and it would be pointless to paralyze this process on account of ideological or moral prejudice.

Now the question is the following: Once foreign capital has earned its profit in Hungary, is there any benefit left for our country? There is no universally valid positive or negative answer to this question, since each case is determined by the concrete conditions of the deal. It would be nonsense to try to attract foreign capital without setting any conditions: "Please be good enough to come and buy up Hungary's state wealth." First of all, Hungary could benefit if the purchase price is reasonable.[24] Furthermore,

[24]The daily papers reported that a British firm bought the controlling stock of Hungary's Ganz Vehicle Factory. The British paid two million pounds in cash. They will cover the remaining amount of the purchase price, ten million pounds, in continuous installments.

This two-million-pound down payment is a shocking sum. I am familiar with the current freehold apartment prices in the area of Boston, Mass. If we take the price of a modest, good quality, seventy-square-meter apartment as a unit, we

Hungary could gain if foreign capital brings along up-to-date equipment and managerial, business, and technical expertise. When the firm is managed by foreign owners, it is often possible to introduce a high degree of organization and discipline. Examples like this are often sufficient to exert a positive influence.

Of course, there is also a need to consider the possible effects of foreign capital on employment, which might well be beneficial. However, here again it is impossible to justify the transaction on the sole basis of this criterion. We must not sell Hungarian state-owned property to foreign owners at any price, merely to preserve the Hungarian jobs at stake. Employment policy disposes of many instruments, and the most advantageous combination of these instruments must be determined case by case.

It may be worth placing an upper limit on the proportion of Hungarian state-owned property that foreigners may buy.[25] But even if limits are placed on foreigners buying up existing state property, no case can be made for any such restriction on direct foreign investment, i.e., in cases where foreign capital sets up a new installation in Hungary, largely with foreign resources.

6. One often hears the bashful argument that the sale of state assets is not meant to produce extra income for the

---

find that the sum paid by the British in cash would buy not more than twelve such apartments. Even if the physical assets of the factory were absolutely worthless, the trade name Ganz would still be worth a multiple of the purchase sum. This kind of squandering of Hungary's state wealth is simply unacceptable.

[25]The South Korean government created an institutional and legal framework for regulating a similar process by setting up a so-called Korea Fund as the only channel through which foreigners could buy Korean property. That example certainly merits careful study.

budget. In fact, some have managed to discredit the idea of a balanced budget to such a degree over the past couple of years that eagerness to collect revenues has become something to be ashamed of. The budget will be discussed in detail in chapter 2. Suffice it here to say that we should accept the fact that the sale of state assets is bound to become a major source of income for the state budget. It logically follows that one cannot be uninterested in the selling price. There are many who just cannot stress enough the need to impose heavy taxes on high incomes. But the same redistributors fail to talk about the price tenants are charged when buying state-owned flats, and they keep skipping the issue of who is entitled, and at what price, to private stocks under the so-called transformation scheme.

Each transaction involving the sale of state assets at a good price, whether to domestic or foreign buyers, releases Hungarian citizens from the need to contribute the same amount to the treasury, either through taxation or inflation. This state revenue, to be sure, is nonrecurrent and not permanent, but it occurs at the best moment, a time when the country is preparing to overcome the greatest difficulties of stabilization.

7. Point 6 gave a brief outline of the fiscal consequences of state property; let us now turn to the monetary consequences. A considerable amount of money has been accumulated by the population, and by the private sector in general. There is no way of telling how much of that is forced saving, i.e., so-called "monetary overhang." In any case this amount of unspent money weighing heavily on the market exerts inflationary pressure. There are various

ways to pump out the unspent money. One such method is the sale of state property.

The actual cash-credit ratio in sales transactions is important, from both the fiscal and monetary vantage points. To come back to our twenty-million-forint example: it is not inconsequential whether the down-payment is two, five, or eight million. Macroeconomic considerations argue for the biggest possible share of cash in the deal. However, an excessively rigid adherence to an exorbitant down-payment could well throw serious obstacles in the way of the sales process. Thus some experimentation on the market will be inevitable.

8. In Hungary the so-called Corporation Law enables a state-owned firm to convert itself into a joint stock company and its shares to pass into the hands of various owners. To my mind the form itself is flexible enough for there to be a favorable transformation, but also for pretended and even quite adverse changes to occur. There is widespread public debate on this issue, with strong criticisms frequently voiced. I would like at this point to make my own position clear.

In my view conversion into a joint stock company ultimately achieves its purpose as long as it leads to a *real* privatization of the firm. Though it may do no harm for shares to pass from one hand of the state into another, I would expect no improvement either.

Now, as far as the passing of shares into private hands is concerned, let me state first of all what I would consider an *incorrect* procedure.

One cannot simply allow the current managers to appropriate the firm and convert themselves from employees paid by the state into owners, or more precisely into owner-managers combining the roles of ownership and management. The new owners should have a free hand in appointing the management. They should be able to keep the old management if they like, or appoint new executives if they prefer. It should also be up to the new owners to decide how to fix executive salaries and financial incentives; that should include the right to offer managers a proportion of the equity at a discount price. But it is inadmissible for the previous managers themselves to choose who the new owners should be or promote themselves to the top of the list of new owners.

As I have mentioned, the employees of the firm may be offered shares at a discount, but I think this option should extend to a small proportion of the shares only. It would not be desirable for the firm's work force as a whole to receive the entire equity (let alone *free,* as the advocates of this solution suggest) so that state property becomes the collective property of the firm's employees. That would amount to the *de facto* introduction of the self-management property format, against which I argue in the next section. Here I would like to refer first to the ethical side of the problem. The wealth embodied by the firm at the moment of ownership transfer has not been created exclusively by that firm's workers; every citizen has contributed through the state investments and state subsidies the firm has received. Nothing justifies a smaller group of citizens now acquiring that wealth as a gift. Moreover, some labor collectives would do very well, since they would receive a thriving firm as a gift, while others would become owners of a heavily indebted, loss-making "negative wealth."

Most important, the prime consideration is not legal entitlement to acquire the property but the ability to run it well. In my view, only private property can supply enough incentive to permanently guarantee an effective use of the resources.

One cannot "calibrate" in advance, by laws or other regulations, how the ownership of the shares is to be distributed. All I can point to is what the desirable trend would be. Let us say the capital of a formerly state-owned firm consists of ten thousand shares. Under the present conditions in Hungary, it would not be advantageous for that capital to be dispersed among ten thousand different shareholders. In that case the previous, quite impersonal state ownership would be replaced by an equally impersonal private ownership. The desirable thing would be a dominant individual shareholder or small group of shareholders capable of acquiring an appreciable stake in the firm (at least 20 or 30 percent of the shares) and thus a decisive say in the appointment and supervision of the firm's executives. This aspiration is consistent with the argument already put forward in favor of the need for visible, "tangible" owners whose private investments (in this case *sizable* shareholdings) give them a strong interest in the firm's success. This dominant group of shareholders could be Hungarian or foreign; the essential requirement is for an effective, direct ownership interest to form.

My belief is that in general, conversion into a joint stock company or some other legal form of private property should be embarked upon only when and where such an individual or group of shareholders has appeared. Once "tangible" owners have appeared and proved, by buying a large number of shares, their willingness to take an appreciable risk, the remaining shares can be sold to other, anonymous buyers. I would have no faith in the success of reversing this course of action, of first selling shares to all and sundry, fragmenting the equity at will, and then hoping for someone who can make his voice heard in the management of the firm.

9. The marketing of state wealth should be a fully public process, and its legal framework should be laid down by law. The law must be circumspect in regulating and limiting the rights and duties of the previous managers. At the time of writing, the legal and organizational framework for the state institutions' handling of privatization are emerging. There is also a need for a parliamentary committee to supervise the execution of the law and exercise independent control over the state organizations responsible for privatization.

The press will play an important role. A genuine business press is needed to provide potential buyers and sellers with information. It is not enough to publish make-believe auction announcements here or there. Business publications should make today's market jungle far more transparent. The public should know the price at which state-owned flats, realties, or factories are sold and bought. There is generally no room for business secrets in cases when the state acts as the seller. Even in exceptional cases when secrecy is justified, the parliamentary committee should still be allowed an inside view.

Besides the specialized business press, the other branches of the media as well as the political opposition will also have an important role to play in exposing occasional abuses.

To sum up, we can say that the sale of state property should *not* be governed by the guiding principle of speed. The "Enough of it, away with it" approach is irresponsible. State ownership has a definite role in places where it can solve certain tasks more efficiently than private ownership. For example, no one would propose to hand over highways to private owners. But even in cases where it is difficult to decide whether state or private ownership is the more efficient, there is a need to carry out specific analyses to explore whether the transaction at issue is efficient in light of the requirements discussed above. State property should be sold to private owners if the deal is advantageous from a macroeconomic point of view, and if there are guarantees that, from the microeconomic perspective, the new owner will do better than the old one. Let us not forget that the prime purpose of privatization is to nurture the *incentive force* private ownership provides.

All these changes will evolve in a prolonged organic process. This process should be energetically accelerated, but it should not be rushed hysterically, nor should it be executed as a sudden operation.

RELATIONS BETWEEN THE STATE AND PRIVATE SECTORS

There can be no "Berlin Wall" between the state and private sectors.[26] Various kinds of relations between them develop, some of them healthy and worthy of support. But

[26]I have borrowed the simile from A. Nagy.

others are harmful, and an attempt must be made to combat them.

It is high time the legal provisions restricting or in some instances prohibiting business dealings between state-owned firms or other state organizations and the private sector were repealed. I am convinced that close economic ties with the private sector can help state-owned firms work more flexibly and fill gaps left by the shortage economy. It would be desirable for private traders in a high proportion of cases to handle transfers of goods produced by a state-owned firm to another state-owned firm that used them. Private traders should be allowed to import state-owned firms' inputs and export their output.

Corruption may arise in all societies at the point of contact between private enterprise and the government sector. Since a state-owned firm is part of the government sector, it is safe to predict that various forms of corrupt practices will arise in the relations between state-owned and private firms. This has been experienced already, and as the private sector strengthens, the cases will become more frequent. There is no watertight way to prevent this damaging and repellent, yet inevitable, accompaniment of the transformation process, but it is worth making strenuous efforts to minimize the problem. That entails suitable legal measures and codes of ethics that distinguish the correct, honest forms of these relations from those legally prohibited and ethically reprehensible. The struggle to enforce the legal regulations and ethical norms must be waged both by the criminal investigative authorities and the general public.

Perhaps more important still is for privatization to proceed successfully. Once the state sector has lost its dominance, the discipline imposed by market competition will tighten, and there will be fewer chances for certain elements of the private sector to gain special advantages through their relations with the state sector. In addition, the economic changes discussed in chapter 2 (a unified system of free prices, a unified convertible currency, the elimination of inflation and the shortage economy) will all help to lessen temptations and opportunities for corruption.

Special mention must be made of those with one foot in one sector and one in the other. Take the case of a worker in a state-owned firm who does repair work in his spare time. His double existence is not objectionable in itself. In fact, understanding must be shown for those who want to retain the security the state sector has offered them so far while augmenting their income in the private sector. Individuals have a sovereign right to decide how long to maintain this double life, which usually entails long working hours and self-exploitation.

But legal measures and the pressure of public opinion must be applied to ensure that no one abuses this dual affiliation. That goes for a worker who feels tempted to expropriate the state-owned firm's means of production or to use them without paying a rent. More serious and more reprehensible still is the case of an executive who plays a double role, acting at once as head of a state-owned firm or institution and as owner, employed manager, or consultant of a domestic or foreign private firm. Strict regulations are needed to define accurately and prohibit conflicts of interest and ethically incompatible dual affiliations.

Such regulations are found in the legal systems of all developed Western democracies; careful study of them would help greatly in preparing similar measures here.

OTHER FORMS OF OWNERSHIP

Three forms will be discussed here:

(a) *Cooperatives.* Cooperatives could play a fairly advantageous role where the following three principles apply: the member is free to enter and exit; upon withdrawal, the member is free to take away not only his own original capital but also his share of the accumulated capital; the cooperative is run by a freely elected, genuine self-government. The cooperative of this kind is in fact a special type of private partnership and is thus not an independent "great sector" of the economy but part of the private sector.

Such cooperatives already exist. I would welcome their spread, although I doubt that they will multiply. Let us wait and see.

I view the various forms of pseudo-cooperatives differently. These bear all the negative characteristics of bureaucratic state ownership. Ideally, these pseudo-cooperatives should transform themselves voluntarily into either genuine cooperatives or other units that operate according to the organizational or legal forms of the private sector. At a minimum, dropping all pretense, pseudo-cooperatives should be openly acknowledged as state property. In any case the Hungarian economy must ultimately rid itself of pseudo-cooperatives.

(b) *Local state ownership.* The status of an economic unit owned by the county, city, or village government (i.e., council in the present state structure) cannot be evaluated with universal validity. The question is: To what degree is the local government able to behave as an authentic owner? In this context there are two other questions to be raised. The first is whether the local legislature is truly representative, and whether it is democratic. If the answer is negative, then the bureaucratic traits that characterized classical nationwide state ownership are bound to re-emerge. The other question concerns the size of the area and of the population administered by a particular local government. A village council would probably perform its duty as owner of a firm within its relatively narrow juris-diction better than would the Budapest municipal council as owner of the large number of firms located in the na-tion's capital. Indeed, the industrial administration of the capital is more likely to exert the type of control practiced by the bureaucratic national ministry.

Only time will tell to what extent local state ownership preserves bureaucratic characteristics of the earlier form of state ownership, and to what extent it engenders genu-ine proprietary interests comparable to those in the private sector. Although I would not exclude the possibility that genuine proprietary interest might emerge, the odds will be unfavorable for a long time to come. Moreover, it is out of the question to expect this form to grow into a huge sector that embraces a considerable part of social produc-tion.

(c) *Labor management.* In this form of ownership em-ployees elect the governing body and the top management of the firm. They also have a say in the day-to-day governance of the firm. In addition, ownership rights are vested either in the work collective as a whole or in individual employees (e.g., through employee shareholding). I do not propose that labor management become the dominant form of ownership, or that today's state sector be transformed into one with labor-management character. The situation is in any case ambiguous: a form of quasi–labor management already prevails in a significant portion of state-owned firms. Several authors have argued in favor of developing this currently ambiguous form into genuine labor management.

The pros and cons of labor management are numerous. In today's Hungary I regard two counterarguments as conclusive. One of them has to do with the enforcement of *wage discipline.* This is in fact an Achilles' heel in the process of dismantling the Stalinist model of the command economy. In a command system mandatory administrative constraints are prescribed both for the level of wages and for the total wage costs of the state-owned firm. Indeed, this is one of the few among the countless plan directives that are enforced with utmost vigor: the observance of wage regulation is rewarded, and their violation punished. The further reform goes toward the liberalization of wage administration, the more quickly wages start to escalate. Bureaucratic compulsion is no longer enforced, but the counterinterest created by private ownership has not replaced it.

The natural interests of the *private* owners run counter to excessive wage raises. The owner starts out from the feeling that each forint he pays out to the employee comes from his own pocket, and that each additional forint is worth it only if it suits his own interest as well (in microeconomic terms, if the marginal productivity of the worker is not less than the wage). On the other hand, this kind of automatic interestedness does not occur in state-owned firms, since the manager does not husband his own money (and is not in the direct employment of private owners either), but merely transfers the money of an impersonal state to his workers. In fact, the manager seeks popularity with the workers, which he can easily obtain by paying higher wages. The most effective way of dissolving tensions inside the firm is to announce a pay increase. In the wake of liberalizing reforms, the state-owned firm operates in a no-man's-land that is neither a command economy, where wage discipline is enforced through bureaucratic means, nor a genuine market economy, where private ownership stimulates this discipline. As a result, wage inflation evolves in all the reform countries. This phenomenon has been observed in China, the Soviet Union, Poland—and in Hungary as well, as the data unambiguously prove.

Labor management can only weaken the position of wage discipline further. Let us examine the situation where the boss is elected by his own staff. Why should he take measures against his subordinates? Why should he play an unpopular part by putting a curb on wages? In fact, the recently introduced elements of labor management in Hungary have contributed to pushing this country toward wage relaxation. This phenomenon is far more marked in Yugoslavia, where labor management has for decades been the basic and officially declared form of ownership, and where, no wonder, wage inflation breaks through at a terrifying rate.

The other major argument against labor management is of a *political* nature. Several opposition forces urged, and Parliament recently codified, a ban on shop-floor party branches, stressing that production should not become embroiled in party wranglings. But if, under present conditions, genuine labor management asserted itself in Hungarian firms, elections of managers and company councils would turn into a stage for party struggles. The various parties or party coalitions would present their own candidates, and launch campaigns for them. Each manager elected by a majority would face the opposition of a minority. In Yugoslavia, which is still a one-party state, this problem is not manifest, since the elections there are in any case not genuine. The Communist party and its subordinate trade union are able to manipulate elections extensively. But if we envisage a genuine multiparty system for Hungary, then we can expect the free election of managers to open the factory doors to party rivalry.

Moreover, the principle of "direct" democracy has been championed primarily by those who wanted it as a substitute for genuine political democracy, or more precisely, for one of its most important constituents: the choice between parties. Those who thought of labor management as a permanent substitute for parliamentary democracy will sooner or later have to see that this is but an inappropriate "forced substitute." And those who opted for labor management out of purely tactical considerations and the lack of a better alternative in the absence of genuine pluralism should now rest assured that we no longer need such ineffective substitutes.

SUMMARY: DUAL ECONOMY

In my opinion we will have to reckon for the next two decades with the *dual* economy that emerged in Hungary over the past ten to twenty years, and with its two constituent parts: the state and the private sectors.

To begin with, the share of the state sector can be decreased only gradually, and we should strive to make it more efficient, but we should not entertain vain hopes. There is no miracle cure that will transform it into a sphere of genuine entrepreneurship. Like it or not, the state sector will retain many negative features. Therefore, we should strive to minimize these negative features through strict financial discipline and appropriate parliamentary supervision, and try to prevent the state sector from siphoning off excessive resources to the detriment of the private sector.

The operating conditions of the private sector must be liberalized in a consistent manner, and its bureaucratic constraints dismantled. Appropriate fiscal and monetary instruments are needed to promote the private sector's fast and energetic development. At the same time, however, we must have no illusions, and recognize that this will be a gradual and protracted development. The proportions between the private and state sectors will shift in the former's favor continually (and one hopes as fast as possible), but there is still a lengthy period of coexistence between them ahead. This symbiosis, though replete with conflicts and frictions, will remain inescapable for a good while.

2

The Surgery
for Stabilization

IN WHAT FOLLOWS, I assume that a new government will be formed as a result of free elections, and that this government will enjoy the confidence of Parliament, and the support of voters. It is beyond the task of this book either to analyze the political conditions necessary for this extremely important development or to consider its prospects. The relationship between economic policy and politics will be examined in the last chapter. The problem I wish to consider here is the following: What stabilization program should be implemented by this new government?

The present study argues that the execution of some of the required tasks should not be prolonged, and cannot be accomplished by a series of small steps. Instead, these measures must be taken *in one stroke*—of course, not necessarily in the literal sense. I would not say that all the necessary regulations must without exception be put into force on the same day. The schedule outlined below is meant to illustrate my point and should thus not be taken as a concrete proposal.

It should be possible to complete a package of measures within one year of the new government's inauguration. The "surgery" must begin on a stated date, and ought to be basically completed within another year. Certain predictable elements of the operation must be made known to the public in advance; others will develop only during the course of the operation. The public must be kept informed on the predictable "postoperative" measures both in the period preceding and also during the surgery.

Obviously, the operation and its key political and economic elements should be agreed upon when forming the government. Together, these elements might provide one of the cornerstones of the new government's economic program. The government apparatus could be given, let us say, a year to work out the details.[27] Naturally, this book

[27]Under any circumstances it will be imperative to involve domestic and foreign experts in this huge undertaking, including people not affiliated with the government apparatus. Let me just highlight one problem in this context.

Nowhere in the world could we find a government that would listen to all the experts of various political and ideological leanings before making a decision. When Britain had a Labour government, it never asked the opinion of the Conservative economists. Instead, the latter expressed their position as a criticism of the government. When Margaret Thatcher came to power, she in turn never employed Labour advisers. The economists to the left of Mrs. Thatcher advised the shadow governments of the opposition parties. Generally speaking, it can be said that *right from the outset* a mutual confidence must exist between a government and the experts it calls upon. They must come to an understanding on at least the fundamental political and ideological issues. Hence it follows that the future government of Hungary should select its advisers from among those Hungarian and foreign economists who wholeheartedly favor the basic principles of its program.

As far as foreign advisers are concerned, I think it is not enough to call upon

cannot undertake to present what will require the work of many experts over a period of several months. My aim here is more modest: I wish to formulate a few key principles as clearly as possible.

Such a stabilization program must range over hundreds of particular issues. The present study should be seen as the first brief outline of such a program. Even in this sketchy form it is far from comprehensive, and skips a number of key issues entirely.

The principles laid down below are all open to question, but I am positive that none can be dodged. It is not at all unlikely that policy speeches during the election campaign will attempt to blur these issues. It is outside my scope to give advice to one or the other party on how to drum up the most possible votes. Nor do I wish to take sides in the ethical and political issue concerning how much of its own dilemmas a political party can be expected to reveal to the electorate in advance, and how much it should be free to leave to later discussion. For example, I will not provide one list of issues to be cleared up during the coalition talks, and another one to be decided in the course of debates within the new cabinet. Consequently, I focus on answering the following question: What should the tasks of the new government be?

To be sure, some critics will not agree with this outline. However, I would like to propose that, for the time being,

---

only those who deal with Hungary "ex officio," like, for example, the officials of the international monetary organizations. I firmly believe that many of the world's best economists will be pleased to serve Hungary with their advice. Some of them will back the future government of Hungary, while there will surely be others to line up behind the various opposition groups.

we set secondary issues aside. At any rate, solutions to these secondary issues will elaborated by larger groups of experts later on. The genuinely basic issues should be highlighted in political and economic debates.

The operation has several components. First I will discuss these components one by one, then argue in favor of their *simultaneous* implementation.

STOPPING INFLATION

The operation is conditioned first and foremost on the understanding that inflation is a grave problem. This is not self-evident to everyone. A fair number of government officials and economists play down this problem, all the more so since inflation is supposedly "in safe hands." In their view fate has ordered inflation for Hungary, thus it is unavoidable and must just be put up with.

Quite conspicuously, neither the opposition parties nor the governing party has made a clear promise to eliminate inflation, if either should come to power after the elections.

Here is a quotation from Minister of Finance László Békesi: "Regrettably, it is not possible to do away with inflation in the coming years. On the one hand, it is the legacy of the earlier voluntaristic economic policy and thus the manifestation of the existing imbalances and inefficiencies. On the other hand, inflation is but the natural fever that accompanies restructuring."[28] I cannot agree

[28]L. Békesi was interviewed by I. Wiesel (1989, p. 19).

105

with this statement. Inflation exists because the acting finance minister and his predecessors acted in a spirit of "Let there be inflation!" Inflation can be stopped *only if* the current finance minister or his successors switch to a policy of "Let there be no inflation!" Inflation is not a natural disaster; it is created by governments or the political powers behind them, and only the governments and political powers can put an end to it.[29]

This statement, albeit forceful, does not have to lead to the extremist and obviously mistaken conclusion that the administration is the *sole* originator and ultimate terminator of the inflationary process. This is a game for many players; inflation is in the hands of all those who play a part in the shaping of the financial processes or in determining prices and wages. In the last analysis, citizens willy-nilly also become prompters of inflation, as they must reckon with future price rises when drawing up their economic plans. This *inflationary expectation* is bound to emerge during an inflationary process, and, regrettably, it has already emerged in Hungary. Beyond a certain point this expectation becomes *self-fulfilling*.[30] If wage earners

[29]The following quote comes from a comment I wrote for a debate on producers' prices in 1986: "The documents presented treat inflation as a kind of impersonal spontaneous process which must be slowed down through anti-inflationary policy. It is my conviction that this is the wrong approach. In both capitalist and socialist countries, the creation of money is ultimately in the hands of the fiscal and monetary authorities. Inflation prevails where the government creates inflation and, in Hungary, an inflationary process has emerged because the government pursues an inflationary policy. As long as the Hungarian government does not change its policy, inflation will not disappear" (J. Kornai [1990]).

[30]A profound analysis of inflationary expectation and other constituents of inflation can be found in F. Vissi (1989). From among the works on inflation in Hungary, I would mention the articles of K. Csoór and P. Mohácsi (1985), M. Z. Petschnig (1986), and T. Erdős (1989).

expect a 20 percent inflation rate, they will strive to gain a wage hike not smaller than 20 percent. Sellers of products or services will aim at a minimum 20 percent price rise. But a distinction must still be made between the "extras" and the "stars" in a multicharacter drama. Whatever the system, the lead in the drama of inflation is played by the government, and more specifically by the financial administration. This obtains even more in the highly centralized socialist economy, where the influence exercised by the government on prices and wages, the credit system, investments, and the other economic processes is incomparably stronger than it is in a capitalist system.

Ultimately, the government controls the banknote press, and it issues additional notes primarily because it wants to cover the gap between governmental expenditures and revenues. Moreover, in a country with a vast state sector, the government resorts to the printing press in order to keep the loss-making firms afloat and to pay the runaway wages. This is why the basic responsibility for inflation rests with the government.

It changes nothing that eminent economists—many of them noted reformists as well—have recommended that the government safely proceed with its inflationary policy. This piece of advice has proved to be mistaken, and each government is responsible for the selection of its own advisers and the inspirators of its policy.

Nor does the recurrent excuse that inflation has overtaken a number of other countries as well provide justification for Hungary's inflation. After all, the defendant before the court cannot to refer to the fact that the offense he is charged with has been committed by scores of other people.

I firmly believe that the rate of inflation in today's Hungary is considerably higher than that shown by official statistics. The official calculation does not assign sufficient weight to the prices in the private sector, especially the price level in the officially unregistered shadow economy, where the increase is much faster than in the state sector. We should not forget that the products and services provided by the private sector account for a large and ever increasing part of total consumption. The report on inflation contains other distortions as well. It is a pity that so far no one has set up and financed a research team whose task would be to calculate inflation *independently* of the Central Statistical Office, which is a governmental body. I would expect this team to impartially rely on well-grounded economic and statistical criteria, and at the same time to heed the opinion voiced by millions of "laymen": inflation is rising faster than official reports will admit.

But let us set aside problems of calculation, and assume instead that the current annual rate of inflation is indeed approximately 15–20 percent. I still consider this a grave problem, for at least two reasons.

1. Inflation descends mercilessly on the population. It leads to perpetual unrest. People see the savings they have scraped together melt away in their hands.

These days we often hear calls for certain *redistributive* measures. But inflation implements a special kind of permanent redistribution, affecting primarily the very poor, salary earners, and pensioners. The widowed and the elderly watch their pensions dissolve in just a few years' time. The purchasing power of the child and family allowances constantly decreases. In the tug-of-war between prices and nominal wages, the losers are those who lack adequate organizational support and political influence, and who are therefore unable to extract wage hikes in order to catch up with price rises, either through slow-downs or open or covert strike threats.

I have read many papers and listened to many political statements on how welfare policy could help the poor. Without taking a position on this question here, I would like to add one comment: It is shocking that most of these statements skip the issue of inflation entirely. I believe that all those who come forward in today's Hungary with a welfare policy program or statement should be obliged to start by spelling out their view of inflation. Do they resign themselves to its continuation without further ado? And more important: do they propose measures that would induce further inflation?

2. Inflation runs counter to the fundamental aims of the transformation of the economic system, mostly by making rational economic calculation impossible. Prices cease to fulfill their signaling function, as the effect of relative shifts in prices are blurred by the general rise in the price level. If goods A and B are substitutes, and good A is gratuitously cheap as compared with good B, then simple economic logic would suggest the raising of the price of good A. Behind this there is the tacit assumption that the price of good B remains unchanged. However, if the price increase of good A is followed by an inflationary price rise of good B, then the relative change in prices cuts no ice at all.

In a market economy efficiency of production shows in the producer's profit. Meanwhile, inefficient production leads to losses, and the loss-making producer is bound to be ousted from the market sooner or later. In this and only this way can the market economy contribute to the efficiency of production. Although this selection process is not realized with 100 percent certainty in a genuine market economy either, the statistical probability of its realization is fairly high. But within an inflationary context, this selection process is undermined, as both efficient and inefficient production are "vindicated." Even if the quality of its work is extremely poor, a production unit can sooner or later cover its costs through a price increase. Those units who want to raise prices are never compelled to admit that perhaps they did not work well, but can always cite rising costs. Even if the ownership conditions allow it, firms' budget constraints cannot be hardened; inflation softens these constraints even in the private sector.

Let us recall the private tradesman in Hungary who does not do his job better than the state-owned firm and who generates dissatisfaction among his clients. One way or another he is still able to set high prices. In this case we should not accuse the tradesman of being greedy and a shark. An economic system cannot be based on self-restraining saints. The problem lies in the fact that the inflationary process creates money in quantities such that the Hungarian customer is able to pay as dearly for the poor services of these private tradesmen as the latter might wish.

This observation is even more applicable to the state sector in today's Hungary. We can in fact witness a dance to a peculiar choreography. The participants are the Price Control Office, which fixes the official price; the producing state-owned firm, which determines the price of those products that can be sold at free prices; the commercial bank, which hands out the money of the state; the National Bank, which puts money in circulation and is said to regulate the allotment of money; the Ministry of Finance, which is in charge of the budget and whose expenses constantly exceed revenues. The sixth, last, and in fact most important participant is the government, and the political powers behind it. Each performer points a finger at the other, and each takes the opportunity during its "inflationary" act to blame the others for their similar role. But hold on—they are all the organs of the same state! Far from being independent of one another, quite the contrary, they together constitute what on p. 60 was called the "governmental sector."

As long as bureaucratic state ownership remains the dominant sector in the economy, it will be impossible to enforce hard budget constraints on the state-owned firms. This fact can be reduced primarily to sociological causes. It bears closely upon those guarantees that this state, willingly or unwillingly, must shoulder in connection with the safe employment of the managers and staff of its own firms. It is practically incapable of deciding to liquidate jobs en masse. Added to this and to the other comparable sociological factors are the effects of inflation: the budget constraint, already soft, is softened further and further by inflation. It is impossible to determine whether the state-owned firm works well or not, and it is likewise impossible to find out the reasons behind rising costs. An analysis of costs would shed light on efficiency only if the price of some of the producing factors was on the rise but not that of others. Similarly, only some but not all of the selling prices should rise. But once there is an overall rise in all costs and in all selling prices, an appraisal of state-owned firms' activity becomes virtually impossible.

Let us look around in the world. The more promarket a politician or economist, the more he is opposed to inflation. Conversely, the more pro-state he is, the less he cares about inflation.

Thus it is one of the basic tasks of the surgery to terminate the inflationary process. Macrosupply and macrodemand must be balanced. As a matter of fact, the gist of the operation is fairly simple. There is a given macrosupply, and facing it is a given macrodemand. On the whole we allow free play to prices. In this situation an equilibrium would come about at some price level. Let us examine the three variables of this relationship more closely.

1. It is not possible to estimate the expected *macrosupply* in advance with any real precision. The process of rearrangement might cut production in certain sectors, while increasing it elsewhere. There is labor shortage in several branches, firms, and regions, which could absorb the labor surplus present in other branches, firms, or regions. The process of rearrangement affords the opportunity to reallocate labor and other material resources. The main thing is this: the better the requirements listed on pp. 38–50 are enforced, the greater the chances for the private sector to prosper. It is highly desirable that the expansion of the private sector counterbalance the contraction of many state-owned firms. In the light of what has been said above, we can assume that macrosupply will settle, perhaps after some wild fluctuations, at its level prior to the

operation. In other words, for the sake of making this brief exposition simpler, we assume that following the first transitional upheaval of the surgery, macrosupply will remain more or less *unchanged* for a while. (Of course, it is to be hoped that it will start to grow again later on.)

2. *Macrodemand* may remain the same as in the beginning of the operation. It may, unavoidably, increase slightly during a short transitional period. But soon after the beginning of the operation, it must be brought firmly under control. A fundamental part of the operation is the strict restriction of macrodemand and all its principal constituents. A later section will address this issue in greater detail.

3. If macrosupply is given and it faces a given macrodemand, then the question arises: What will be the *average macro price level* at which supply and demand will reach equilibrium? I am afraid no one can tell for certain what it would be. There is no way to calculate precisely the overall effect of the complicated circular price and cost spillovers.[31] The package of measures I propose bears no resemblance to the one that has repeatedly been put into practice in the Soviet Union and once or twice in the smaller socialist countries of Eastern Europe. Those packages boiled down to an effort to work out in advance all the simultaneous price and cost effects. In our case there is no need for the prior determination of millions of prices in the offices of the price authorities, as they will duly emerge by themselves out on the market.

---

[31]Meanwhile, we must still do our best to predict the processes that can be expected during and after the operation by applying up-to-date scientific means. Here the models of modern macroeconomics can be utilized.

In all likelihood the operation would finally bring about a considerable rise in the average price level as compared with the current level. This, however, could remain a non-recurrent development, provided that from the very beginning the government sticks to a steadfast anti-inflationary policy. The price rises accompanying the operation will not necessarily lead to inflation. Should the rise in the price level exceed the average rate of inflation in the preoperation years, this would still not have to result in accelerating inflation later. We must understand clearly that inflation is a *dynamic* process; it is but the spiral of increases in prices, wages, and other cost factors. If this spiral were cut and the reproduction of macro excess demand done away with, there would be a good chance to eliminate inflation. This is what we must accomplish.

RESTORATION OF BUDGETARY EQUILIBRIUM

A fatalistic approach to balancing the budget prevails: a sense of inability to act and a feeling that this fiscal disequilibrium is unavoidable.

Foreign examples abound. One of these is the grave and persistent budget deficit of the United States. If the Americans are not able to overcome this problem, how can we Hungarians surmount it? I consider this reasoning illogical. The situation in the United States differs radically from that of Hungary; the condition of the U.S. budget has no relevance whatsoever to that of the Hungarian budget. But speaking of the Americans, let me say briefly that almost all economic and political groups in the United States see the budget deficit as a grave ill. However, when it comes to finding a cure, varying opinions surface both among the public and in the Congress, which represents the American population. Some groups feel inclined to raise taxes, while others emphatically reject this option and show a willingness instead to shoulder the negative consequences of the deficit.

In addition to the United States, there are several other capitalist countries where budget deficits were or are a grave concern. But it is also noteworthy that a number of capitalist countries (for example, Switzerland, Finland, and Singapore) have been able to operate their economy for many years without running a budget deficit.

The expedience of a balanced budget and the possibilities of reestablishing equilibrium in case of a deficit are prime bones of contention among economists in the West. It is clearly not the task of the present book to pass judgment on the different budget policies of the modern capitalist countries.[32] A negative statement will suffice here: The history of capitalism does *not* support the claim that it is *impossible* to preserve budgetary equilibrium, nor does it bear out the idea that a balanced budget is an unacceptable and unachievable goal. It is time to stop pointing fingers at modern capitalism and turn instead to our own situation.

I believe that in the course of the stabilization operation, budgetary balance must be fully restored by means of

[32]There were periods when, prompted by Keynesian economic policy, deficits were created on purpose. The aim was to promote economic upswing through an artificially created excess demand. This had dubious results.

certain drastic measures. To be able to cover expenditures out of revenues after so many years of budgetary imbalance is an opportunity not to be missed.

The need to cut public expenditures is a recurrent point in debates and political statements on the balance of the budget. I fully agree with calls for reduced spending, but I do not want to dwell at this point on the related tasks. If we take into account the elimination of subsidies, we still face certain budgetary expenditures needed for covering the costs of the state administration and the armed forces, servicing the foreign debt of the government and the state sector, and economic and welfare expenses. The core of my proposal is as simple as this: the amount of taxes collected annually should be set to cover those given annual expenditures. When preparing for the operation, we must not entertain the doubtful prospect of higher than expected expenditure cuts. True enough, this approach might better serve the popularity of a politician, since people in general lean toward those who speak up for the reduction of state expenditures instead of announcing a revenue increase. However, the problem cannot be solved by holding a popularity contest. The plan of the operation should determine the amount of revenues necessary to cover expenditures unambiguously and safely. It would be preferable for revenues to slightly exceed the required amount rather than to have just one forint less than what is needed.

All this necessitates the radical reshaping of the tax system. At the moment, the Hungarian tax system is but a troubled brew of the paternalistic redistribution of a socialist economy, the fiscal impotence of a destitute Third

World country, and the refined progressive tax system of a Scandinavian welfare state. Those who elaborated Hungary's new tax regulations and managed to sell them to the economic leadership, to most of the deputies in Parliament, and to part of the public have gotten their way by suggesting that Hungary play at being a little Sweden. As a bitter joke has it in Budapest, we now have Hungarian wages minus Swedish taxes. Regrettably, a number of incompetent and superficial Western observers have also been taken in; they were inclined to see the new Hungarian tax system as a token of this country's "Westernization."

When we sit down to draft a new tax system, as part of the stabilization operation, we should start by brushing away the existing system—if not in reality, then at least in our imaginations. Let us go back to square one and reconsider systematically the underlying principles of the new tax system.[33] I do not strive for completeness; I emphasize only those principles that are particularly important to take into account in the course of the current revision of the tax system and in the preparation of the stabilization operation.[34]

1. Taxes should be collected where they are "seizable," giving preference to the technically simplest forms of taxation. This point, seemingly technocratic and devoid of eth-

[33]This book does not take up the question of how these proposals, if accepted, should be translated into the language of tax laws. Whether we should modify the existing tax laws or instead create a "tabula rasa" and supersede the old laws with new ones is mostly a legal matter. For purposes of *conceptualization,* it is expedient to start out from a tabula rasa.

[34]Those wishing for a more general survey of the basic principles of taxation might consult, for example, the books of R. A. and P. B. Musgrave (1980) and J. Stiglitz (2nd ed., 1986).

ical significance, actually suggests serious ethical and political requirements.

We are dealing with Hungary, not Scandinavia. In the past the more loudly official propaganda declared that the state belonged to the people, the less people believed it. Nowadays, people in general consider it a laudable act, rather than something to be ashamed of, if someone defrauds the state, appropriates its wealth, or shuns his own obligations. Those who refrain from this kind of behavior are seen as dupes. Teenagers everywhere boast about cheating by not paying the fare on the publicly owned tram. In the past decades this kind of cheating has become typical behavior in Hungary even among adults. It would be irrational to expect this conduct to change overnight, no matter how great a political change takes place. In particular, behavior cannot be expected to change immediately once elected representatives of the people assume control over the treasury. No one can predict how much time this turn in the public spirit will take. We can safely assume only that more than two or three years will be required.

Consequently, when we contemplate budget revenues, we should be prepared to face the fact that many citizens will try hard to dodge taxes. Within the limits of the possible, they will understate their incomes. People do the same in the West, although the intensity may vary according to countries. Presumably, this problem is more common in the southern part of Europe than in the north, although tax morality is on the wane in Scandinavia as well. In the Hungarian case there is an additional factor: a considerable part of the private sector still belongs to the shadow economy, and it will voluntarily emerge from the shadow and into the light only after some time. Chapter 1 gave a detailed list of the requirements necessary for this to take place.

Under these conditions, what is the meaning of the tax system's heavy reliance on voluntary tax returns?

The first possible answer: The government is building castles in the air. It is deceiving itself by counting on revenue, most of which it will never be able to collect.

The second possibility: The government is taking a reasonable line and is building into the system the possibility that citizens will try to cheat in any event. This approach is not unfounded, but it is quite dishonest. This means that the deputy in Parliament who passes the tax laws, the official who executes these laws, and the defrauder himself exchange significant glances: "We pretty well know that all those decent dupes will pay their taxes, and we do not even expect to collect taxes from those who are determined to shirk it."

Finally, the third possibility: Instead of the exchanging of significant glances, a resolute decision is taken to exact personal income taxes. But what can the state do in a country where tax morality is very low? Exactly what the tax authority tries to do now, although inconsistently. It tries to spy upon the taxpayers: it investigates income sources and spending patterns; it encourages people to denounce to the police any conspicuously prosperous neighbors who may be suspected of not paying their taxes properly. The ultimate solution would be an Orwellian system. In each household there would be a tax inspector who would keep a constant check on the family's daily earnings and expenditures. In this case it would surely pay to promise "head money" to the inspectors, and of course to duly reward them for each collared citizen.

The mere possibility of this system is enough to horrify anyone who favors individual autonomy, wants citizens to be free to dispose of their own money, and requires full respect of privacy.[35]

Thus, point 1 turns out to be much more than a merely technical one. Without attempting to give a prescription to all tax authorities of the world, let me state that today Hungary needs a tax system able to evade the dilemmas described above. This system should neither test citizens'

[35]I hear again references to the practice in the West. But there it took decades or even centuries to develop a parliamentary democracy that established confidence in the relationship between the citizen and the state. In the West the interference by tax authorities in the private life of the citizen is limited by laws, and it is also possible for the citizen to go to court to challenge any kind of state action. And still, under those conditions, the tax authority all too frequently abuses its power.

The brutality with which the world-famous film director Ingmar Bergman was carried away from a filming session to face a charge of tax fraud before a court of law is well known. This happened in Sweden, a country often cited as a model. Bergman was crushed by the events; he emigrated and worked for years in voluntary exile, although he remained strongly attached to his homeland. Many years later he was rehabilitated, but the loss caused to Bergman and as a result to universal human culture by an unscrupulous tax bureaucracy is irrevocable.

It is beyond the task of this book to draw conclusions about the tax system of Sweden or of any other Western parliamentary democracies. However, it remains certain that the likelihood of similar cases happening in Hungary is remarkably higher, provided that a personal income tax system is consistently enforced. And here lies the fundamental moral dilemma: Which sin is greater? Shall we punish one hundred people, admitting that there might be one innocent person along with the ninety-nine guilty, just to prevent the ninety-nine from escaping? Or shall we let the ninety-nine make off just to prevent even a single innocent individual from suffering? Personally, I adhere firmly to the latter solution.

loyalty, nor force legislators and the bureaucracy to decide whether or not to poke their noses into the private sphere of the household. At the same time, this system should be efficient enough to collect the taxes necessary for the maintenance of the state. The tax categories should be as *impersonal* as possible. If everything goes well, democracy will become consolidated in Hungary, most Hungarian citizens will again become attached to their state, and all the necessary conditions will be ensured for the smooth operation and legality of the private sector. Then and only then can we begin to consider a general personal income tax.

2. The tax system should be as *neutral* as possible. Apart from justifiable exceptions, the state should not reward or punish through the tax system. If the national or local legislature decides to subsidize someone for welfare, cultural, or other social considerations, it should do so openly.[36] Separate items should be reserved on the *expenditure side* for this purpose, instead of using tax reductions on the *revenue side.* I do not wish to join the ongoing debate about whether to provide textbooks free of charge to every schoolchild. Parliament has the right to decide on such policies, of course, conscious of the fact that allocating the necessary funds will mean expenditure cuts elsewhere, or additional taxes. Once the deputies vote for the free distribution of textbooks, the expenses incurred should be listed on the expenditure side of the budget, under the heading "educational expenses" and among the

---

[36]A certain form of financial assistance given to the needy is called "negative income tax" in Western literature. The above train of thought is obviously not averse to granting this negative income tax, as it is neither an award nor a punishment. In other words, it does not serve as an "incentive."

paragraphs on "cultural subsidies." The sums at issue should in no way be lost in the mists of reduced tax rates for textbook publishers or book distributors.

Accordingly, the concrete meaning of point 2 is that whatever the tax category applied may be (consumption tax, payroll tax, and so on), the tax rate should be *rigorously uniform*. We must put an end to arbitrary tax exemptions for certain products, services, activities, or social groups. We need welfare, health, and cultural policies, all of which require state subsidies, but the money for this should not be raised through the manipulation of tax rates. The would-be political powers should declare that they will not yield to lobbying, pressure, or threats, and that they will not depart from the principle of uniform tax rates.

Incidentally, this principle is of prime importance from the point of view of the market economy as well. There will be no genuine market without genuine prices. Biased tax exemptions are bound to be incorporated into the price system, and will prevent us from having a clear conception of the real cost of each product. And since all elements of the price system are interdependent, each and every price will appear in the form of costs in the overall set of prices and wages. Ultimately, differentiated and chaotic taxes distort the price system. True adherents of the market economy should thus insist on uniform tax rates, i.e., a tax system that is as neutral as possible.

3. There is no need to make the tax system progressive. I am well aware that this idea shocks many in Hungary, where the vast majority sides with progressive taxation.

However, I still feel compelled to take this view.

Income distribution is primarily an *ethical* issue. This is why no one is entitled to claim that it is possible to decide what is a "correct" income distribution on purely rational grounds. Some people attach an intrinsic value to *equality* of income and welfare. These people would rather resign themselves to a lower level of efficiency or a smaller national income in exchange for an even distribution of products (or at least for as even a distribution as possible). Like all other ethical standpoints, this one is also metarational, i.e., it brooks no rational counterargument. All I can do at this point is to state that I do not go along with this egalitarian requirement. It gives me no moral satisfaction to see above-the-crowd people being pulled down to the lowest common denominator. My approach treats the question of what should be done for the good of the poor, the handicapped, the destitute, and the disabled separately from the problem of whether more prosperous people should be deprived of part of their earnings and properties.

"Equality" is a complex moral value of several dimensions. I can fully identify with several of its ingredients. Equality before the law; rejection of privileges based on social extraction, color of skin, religious affiliation, or gender; equal entitlement to basic human rights—these are some of the egalitarian principles that feature prominently in my set of values. The acceptance of *these* values is fully compatible with the rejection of the equalization of material incomes.

At the same time, I go along with those who wish to enforce the principle of *social justice in distribution.* Of

123

course, this leaves open the question of how the notion of "social justice" is defined. One conception to which I also subscribe holds that a distribution system is fair only if it ensures continuous improvement in the material situation of the least well-off strata of society in the long run.[37]

Let me stress that this principle is a *dynamic* requirement. It does not inquire about the precise share the least well-off receive from the given national income at a given moment. Consequently, this is not a static redistributive requirement: it does not measure, in the sense of a cross section, the situation of the poor in comparison with the wealth of the rich. This requirement has a temporal dimension, as it compares the situation of the poor today with that of tomorrow. It calls for a system in which this temporal comparison produces a favorable result. The poor should not be predestined to lead a life of desperation and hopelessness; instead, they should feel positive about the promise of a steady improvement.[38]

Of course, this requirement is not meant to indicate a monotonous improvement taken in a mathematical sense. It does not hold out the promise that the situation of all poor people will steadily improve week by week. But it does hold out the promise that the financial circumstances of all the needy will perceptibly improve in the foreseeable future, i.e., within each one- or two-year period. The society that does not guarantee this is unjust.

---

[37]This is a necessary, but in itself not sufficient, condition of social justice.

[38]This is a *dynamic reformulation* of the criterion of justice suggested by Rawls, presented in the present book in a simplified way. For more detailed treatment, see J. Rawls (1971), R. Nozick (1974), A. Sen (1988), and J. Kis (1986).

The requirement leaves open the question of what the income distribution should look like among the remaining members of society, who are not at the lower end of the scale. This issue again has many ethical aspects, but these fall beyond the scope of the present book. I stress here only those aspects that bear closely upon the subject at hand. Income distribution should give the *strongest possible incentive* to the increase of the total income of society, as this is the sine qua non for a *steady* increase in the income of the poorest. The improvement of the lot of the poorest through redistributive means offers only finite prospects. Take a piece of bread and divide it equally among a group of people consisting of N people: each person receives a share of 1/N. The justice requirement stated above can be fulfilled only if the piece of bread to be divided grows larger and larger. Consequently, the requirement of social justice is inseparable from the requirement of incentive. The politician or economist who leaves this requirement out of consideration is a hothead at best or a demagogue at worst. And this leads us on to the last general requirement related to the tax system.

4. The tax system should contain *no counterincentive* to the improvement of economic performance and the increase of investments. It should not impose a progressive tax on those who are ready to sacrifice part of their free time to work overtime or extra, and it should not compel them to lie to the state by disguising this fact. The tax system should not punish those who, instead of hiding their money under the mattress, deposit it in a bank in order to earn interest.

Irrespective of the actual date on which the draft of the

Tax Law goes before Parliament, I recommend that the deputies always keep in mind the following question: What effect will the tax have on performance, production, and investments? Should this effect turn out to be negative in any of these cases, then they had better not pass the law. Such a Tax Law would be detrimental to the future development of Hungary's economy. It would also be harmful from the point of view of welfare (see my arguments under point 3 concerning assistance to the poor).

Finally, it would also be disadvantageous from a strictly fiscal point of view. There are well-known studies on fiscal policy that use theoretical models and empirical calculations to point out important relationships between tax rates and revenues. It is the wrong fiscal policy to levy a high tax rate on a stagnating or ominously sluggish national income in the false hope of collecting a high tax revenue. If, on the contrary, the finance ministry avoids the counterincentive created by excessively high tax rates, it will be much more successful in increasing its revenues, and once it clears the way for the rapid growth of national income, it will be able to collect more in tax even at a lower tax rate.

After this brief survey of the main principles of taxation, let us now examine in more concrete terms the tax categories needed for putting this system into practice. It is not the task of the present book to work out in full detail concrete taxation formulas. I only wish to make it plain which tax categories I think should account for the bulk of the budget's revenues given the conditions in present-day Hungary.

(a) Most important is the linear *consumption tax,* or more precisely its most up-to-date form, some kind of value-added tax.[39] The application of this tax could rely the most on the current tax system. But it should differ from the present system in that uniformity should be enforced with unswerving consistency.[40]

My proposal to abolish the progressive income tax is often countered with the suggestion to reintroduce at least some progressivity via differentiated value-added tax rates; for example, higher rates on luxury goods and lower rates on goods consumed mainly by low-income households. I do not reject this idea unconditionally, since I respect the requirements of fairness in distribution. Yet we must be aware of the potentially great disadvantages. The differentiated tax might open the door to pressures for lower tax rates in various specific instances and to a quick reemergence of price distortions. Therefore, in the first few years uniform rates might be preferable. At a later stage, when a rational, market-clearing price structure has evolved, tax rate differentiation for the sake of distributive justice might be considered anew.

(b) There should be a single linear (nonprogressive)

---

[39]The proposed tax system lays a tax primarily on the *consumption* of income; consequently, the nonconsumed income remains tax-exempt, thereby indirectly encouraging saving and investment.

The idea that the income tax puts those who save at a disadvantage has its roots in the works of John Stuart Mill. The same idea was raised with great emphasis later by Irwing Fisher (1942). For the advantages and disadvantages of the consumption tax, and especially the value-added tax, see R. A. and P. B. Musgrave (1980).

[40]I would not object to well-considered, rare exceptions for other reasons, for example, a special tax levied on alcoholic beverages, provided that Parliament accepts it while fully aware that this is but a paternalistic intervention.

By the way, the effectiveness of a high tax in fighting alcoholism is arguable. It remains certain that overtaxation, like administrative curbs, cannot eliminate alcoholism. Instead, it leads to evasion on the part of the legal, taxpaying distilling industry and to the emergence of illegal distillation.

payroll tax. All employers who pursue their activity legally should be subject to payroll tax for any kind of remuneration they pay out to their employees.

I consider it utterly prejudicial to introduce any kind of progression in the taxation of earned incomes. On what ground does the state punish, for example, those nurses, teachers, workers, or clerks who are willing to sacrifice their free time and work overtime?

My criticism here is directed not merely at the extension of working hours, but also at the practice of differentiation according to the quality of work done. Let us assume that the work done in job A is worth three times more than that performed in job B, because the former requires better skills, involves greater responsibility, or is physically more exhausting. Now what is the use of paying worker A four times the wage of worker B in gross just to reach the 3 to 1 ratio in their net wages after the deduction of the progressive income tax? This is but a completely superfluous taxation procedure, which only puts additional burdens on payroll and tax clerks.[41]

(c) There should be a single linear (nonprogressive) *profit tax*. The rate of this tax should be strictly uniform. Consequently, the same tax rate should be applied to the profits of all legally registered firms, irrespective of whether they are owned by the state or by private individuals, or whether the owner is a Hungarian or a foreigner.

In connection with categories (b) and (c), one might

[41]This in fact became obvious when this senseless procedure had to be performed *in reverse* prior to the introduction of the personal income tax, when former incomes were "grossed up."

disapprove of the fact that these fail to levy taxes on those incomes that are generated *outside* the "normally" registered, tangible firms. This may well be considered unfair, since it is quite possible that excessively high incomes come from this very sphere, which in turn evades taxation.

This dilemma, of course, is quite real. But let me suggest a pragmatic approach. While weighing the problem carefully, we should not just throw all the "invisible" incomes into a single basket, but should instead execute the following classification for the sake of analysis.

i) Citizens make money or get payment in kind by engaging in diverse forms of moonlighting: some market fruit grown in their gardens, the secretary does some extra typing, the translator translates, the schoolgirl baby-sits, and so on. The whole society benefits from this, as these activities all add to the national income. Now let us resign ourselves to the prospect that this kind of income remains untaxed. What I have said above applies to these incomes to a perhaps even greater degree: it is not possible to assign an inspector to each citizen just to keep an around-the-clock watch over his earnings. The practical concession that we resign ourselves to the tax-exemption of these incomes is at the same time an incentive to increase the supply of these kinds of products and services. Today, when "formal" production is all but stagnating, it benefits all of us if active and self-sacrificing people turn out more products and services for society.

We need to take special care not to maintain the bizarre regulations that levy taxes on tips and gratuities. In Hungary, for example, not only waiters and taxi drivers, but also physicians and nurses in public health service and salespersons in shops selling goods in short supply receive some sort of gratuities. On the one hand, taxies levied on gratuities compel those who receive tips or gratuities literally to exact payment that in fact is not their due. On the other hand, those who earn high sums are able to disguise as much as they want. Consequently, such a tax law simply serves to further undermine the authority of the legal system.

ii) My proposals are not meant to exempt plant-size private enterprises from paying profit tax. The "gray zone" of the private sector, i.e., the one whose activity is not severely persecuted by law but is not fully legal either, has been rather wide to date. The general spirit of the present book suggests that the private firm and its owner step into the fully legal sphere openly and without fear or shame. In fact, what we offer the private entrepreneur is an "exchange deal." He can have legal protection and guaranteed enforcement of private contracts; in return, just as the more easily controllable state-owned firm, he has to pay taxes. It can be assumed that there are individuals or groups within the private sector who would opt for remaining in the gray or black zone. Now these people have to reckon with the possibility that they might be prosecuted by the law, among other reasons, for tax fraud. Moreover, they should also be aware that if they are cheated by their contracting parties, be these state-owned firms or private enterprises, buyers, or sellers, they will have no protection under the law. They will likewise lose the opportunity to sue any official organization that happens to treat them badly.

And, what is more, customers of the gray zone will also have to run a similar risk. They will not, for example, have any guarantees or right to restitution in case of breach of contract. The more successful the country will be in ensuring the security and authority of private property (see pp. 34–57), the more worthwhile it will be for the private sector to come out of the dark, and consequently to accept the obligation of paying taxes. This is the only realistic way to tax the private sector.

And here I wish to return again to the arguments against a progressive income tax.

Under existing conditions in Hungary, it is on the whole illusory to entertain the idea of a progressive tax. In point of fact, the burden of the income tax falls only on those whose incomes are "scannable" in the official records. And among these people, taxation puts the heaviest burden on those whose economic, social, and political status is not strong enough to let them shift this burden to others. Those people whose incomes are recorded but whose bargaining position is strong are able to *de facto* "gross up" their incomes by the amount of the tax. The employer cannot but pay the gross wage for which the employee is willing to work. In this way the employee ultimately shifts his tax burden to others. Nor does the progressive tax affect those private entrepreneurs who are able to pass the tax burden to the customers through price increases. And finally, the least afflicted are those the populist tax propaganda says should be burdened the most: the recipients of "invisible incomes."

Now let us return to our survey of the budget's revenue side.

(d) Although it is not a tax category in the technical sense, I will mention the *customs duty* here. If customs duties are indispensable to cover budget expenditures, then their magnitude should be small, so as to distort the price level as little as possible. And the most important thing is that a uniform linear customs duty should be levied on all kinds of cross-border imports. (I do not want to enter into the question of whether Hungary wants to inflict surcharges or dispreferential customs duties on certain import deals, depending on the country of origin.) Apart from justified exceptions, there should be no differentiation among the customs tariffs on various products.[42] The customs tariff should be strictly uniform, irrespective of whether the importer is declaring coffee or computers, cars or children's wear, so as to avoid distortions in the relative prices.

It is possible to compile a reasonably limited duty-free quota for tourists, but all items above this quota should be subject to duty. However, private individuals should all be free to import whatever kinds of goods they wish, and in unlimited quantities, provided they pay the uniform customs duty. Here is an up-to-date example. Private individuals should be granted the right to buy an unlimited number of computers with hard currency they previously obtained on the private hard currency market, and should be free to import this equipment. Once an individual pays the uniform duty, he should be granted the right to sell his imported computers at free prices, i.e., for as much as the buyer is willing to pay.

The right to free import by private persons is the unconditional legal right of citizens. The source of the foreign currency used for imports is another question. No eco-

[42]The support of domestic infant industries may require protective tariffs. We will return to this question in connection with the discussion of production subsidies.

nomic problems arise as long as the citizen obtains his foreign currency on the private market. It is imperative that a realistic, uniform exchange rate finally be developed during the stabilization operation, together with the introduction of convertibility. Of course, in this event, it will also become the enforceable civic right of every Hungarian citizen to exchange Hungarian forints freely for convertible foreign currency at the state bank.

Although our major theme at present is the stabilization operation, it is worth mentioning a further question related to private imports: What should be done in the period before the stabilization operation has been fully implemented and a realistic exchange rate, as well as genuine convertibility, has been assured? From my point of view it does not make sense in the face of an unrealistic exchange rate for the state bank to guarantee large quantities of foreign currency to every citizen as a matter of his civic rights. The convertibility of the forint at the state bank should become a civic right as a result of the stabilization operation—but this must be supported by the proper economic conditions: rational free prices (pp. 145–154) and a rational hard currency exchange rate (pp. 155–158).

And now a few more general comments on these basic principles concerning the revenue side of the budget.

I did not aim at completeness in enumerating the above cluster of revenues. There might well be a few more sources (fees, for example).[43] However, when it comes to working out the operation schedule, it is *vital* that the sum total of the main sources of revenues (consumption tax,

[43]This book leaves open several problems of the tax system, such as the issue of the property tax, the taxation of the self-employed, and so on. Of course, a new tax system must solve these problems as well.

payroll tax, profit tax, and import duty) cover the actual expenditures. The scalpel must not shake in the hand of the surgeon. The tax rates must be set in such a manner that they will cover the expenditures with complete certainty.

Quite a few shockingly dilettantish comments were made in earlier debates on the revenue side of the budget in the press, in political speeches, and during the parliamentary debate over the state budget and the Tax Law. Some remarks gave the impression that the whole issue boiled down to the question "Who will foot the bill? The budget or the population?" Greedy fiscal bureaucrats feel victorious whenever they manage to pass the buck to the population, and the "defenders of the people" are likewise triumphant if they manage to push the buck back to the budget. In the meantime, they all lose sight of the fact that in either case it is the population who has to bear *all costs,* except, of course, for that slice the state temporarily manages to charge to foreign sources, in return for further external indebtedness. In the long run this debt will have to be paid by the population, by present and future generations. The issue under consideration is never a *choice* between the budget and the population. Instead, the question always concerns *the distribution of the burdens* among the various strata of the population, and also among present and future generations.

Another question concerns the *form* in which the population is supposed to cover these costs. There are different courses to choose from: people might pay prices implicitly covering the tax (consumption tax); they might be confronted with a specious solution in which their employer seems to pay the tax (payroll tax); they might be taxed indirectly through inflation; and so on. But whatever the method, it is the population who pays the bill. Now, since there is no getting away from this situation, then at least I would suggest that this taxation procedure be executed in the simplest and most efficient way possible. If my proposals were put into practice, we could dismantle the bulk of the newly created tax bureaucracy. This in itself would be a gain.

Now we will turn our attention to the *expenditure side.* The expenditure must be considered a given sum at the moment of the operation. There are only two items that must be eliminated from the budget.

The first item is the *budgetary price subsidies* of certain consumer goods. The process of removing parts of these subsidies has been going on for a while now, and it is possible that further partial measures will be implemented prior to the start of the actual operation. But whether the process has fallen far short of declared targets or progressed quite far, at the time of the surgery this painful task must be definitively and completely accomplished. No excuse for not taking the medicine should be allowed, whatever the counterindications might be.

I am a zealous believer in the idea that the state should act in a humane way: it is not only the right but also the obligation of Parliament to adopt welfare policy expenditures suited to the potential of the country. But these expenditures should not occur in the form of price subsidies, because the subsidized prices help those who stand in need as well as those who do not. I also approve of the idea that the state, along with other institutions and private individuals, should patronize culture. But this again should not be done in the form of subsidized prices. If we can afford it, then let us give book vouchers to the students; but the book prices should remain realistic, i.e., they should cover the costs and the profit. There is no need to subsidize the book purchases of those who can afford to buy books at market prices.

And most important: at the current economic level in Hungary, there is nothing to justify the subsidization of foodstuffs. The current standard of economic development in this country is more than sufficient to ensure that each citizen can fill his or her biological demands. Now why should the country keep food prices artificially low and thereby give special grants to those who otherwise would be able to pay the real market price? What is the use of making Hungary a laughingstock in the eye of the Austrian tourists, who flock here to buy meat for a fraction of the Austrian price? I fully appreciate the fact that segments of our society can hardly make ends meet even at today's food prices. These groups, which include retired people with meager pensions or multiple disadvantages, must be supported directly, through pecuniary assistance, help in kind, or restaurant vouchers, but definitely not through an absurd distortion of the price system.

The other item to be eliminated from the budget is the huge amount of all kinds of *production subsidies*, save a couple of clearly defined exceptions. This is precisely the right moment to put an end to two decades of argument about loss-making state-owned firms and large agricultural cooperatives. The two admissible exceptions are the following:

(a) Transitional support, meant to help over the worst of the postoperation shock.

(b) Initial support, to be extended to infant industries or branches. Familiar arguments abound in the literature in support of protecting infant ventures in order to protect national production. To be sure, there is a need to wait until Hungarian pioneers obtain practical knowledge and reach economies of scale. This kind of support, either in the form of state subsidies or of protective tariffs, however, should have a fixed deadline; if the new producer fails to gather strength by then, support should be withdrawn. There is no need to keep nonviable organizations alive by artificial means.

To sum up: The operation must reestablish budget equilibrium. This is absolutely needed to eliminate inflation. When on p. 106 I maintained that inflation is the product of the government in power, I referred mainly (although not exclusively) to the fiscal aspects of the processes that fuel inflation. The means to finally restore budgetary balance are in the hands of the government in power and the deputies in Parliament who determine and enact the government's revenues and expenditures.[44]

In the postoperation period it is important to maintain and even increase efforts aimed at slashing budget expenditures. The more successful these efforts are, the greater the possibility for reducing tax rates. A tax cut would surely increase the government's popularity. But beware:

[44]This, of course, also means that Parliament must at long last be given an insight into the budget; the true magnitude of the deficit must not be covered up by financial tricks. Parliament should have a real grasp of military expenditures and so on.

during the operation we cannot spend in advance would-be and still uncertain cuts.

MANAGING MACRODEMAND

Without aiming at completeness, I wish to discuss only a few ideas, and above all highlight the dangers that might jeopardize the success of the stabilization program.

At the moment of the operation, the amount of money held by the private sector is constant. Therefore, there is no threat of purchasing power getting out of hand. As I have already stressed, the credit quota supplied by the state-owned banking sector to the private sector must be fixed. On the one hand, these credits must reach the private sector upon demand, i.e., the state sector must be prevented from siphoning them off. On the other hand, it is also necessary to keep the private sector from overstepping these limits during the critical first phase of the operation. Once the private sector is on its feet, it is possible to increase the supply of credit in proportion to the growth of its credit demand. Meanwhile, the private sector units should be encouraged to create ever more extensive credit linkages among themselves, and it is also imperative to create the legal infrastructure required by these contacts.

The state budget was discussed in detail in the previous section. Let us presume that the principles described there are all realized, i.e., that the demand created by the state budget is strictly restrained.

The real danger lies in the eventuality that demand by state-owned firms (and also by the sector of quasi-state-owned large cooperatives) runs away. Recall that on p. 64 I proposed regulations to curb the spending of state-owned firms. Here I offer this proposal again, while emphasizing that the real test for this curb will be the stabilization operation itself. In the past decades, financial authorities have pursued a policy of strict *monetary restriction.*[45] This effort was only partly successful. It managed to prevent excessive runaway macrodemand and the outbreak of a hyperinflation as occurred in Yugoslavia and Poland—although even as it is, we have 15–25 percent inflation, which is already too high. The restriction was accompanied by many kinds of spasms and undesirable side effects; often it prevented the increase of production and investment even in areas where it would have been truly profitable.

Given that up to now real interest rates have been unrealistically low (i.e., slightly or strongly negative), it was not possible to develop a truly rational restrictive monetary policy. However, at least this experience has shown that it is *possible* to enforce monetary restriction under our conditions, although it would be desirable that this policy be carried out in a more prudent and well-grounded fashion in the future. One of the first and most important instruments of this policy will be high, positive real interest rates on lending.

In any case the recent history of monetary restriction provides an instructive illustration of the necessity for implementing the various parts of the stabilization program *simultaneously.* Monetary restriction, thus far carried out

[45]In this connection, see E. Várhegyi (1989).

in the absence of the other necessary complementary measures, has not produced the desired results: it has not brought an end to inflation and to the practice of artifically keeping alive low-efficiency firms. As a result, the principle of monetary restriction has unfortunately been discredited in the eyes of many, so that it will be harder to implement in the future.

We must be fully aware of the phenomena that go along with the restriction of macrodemand. Here I point out only two.[46]

1. In the classical socialist command economy, credit supply was the monopoly of the state bank system. "Commercial credit," i.e., the *granting of mutual credit among state-owned firms,* was strictly forbidden. However, in the wake of "market socialism"–type reforms and the partial liberalization of state-owned firms, interfirm credit not only occurred suddenly but also became general in all socialist reform countries. This type of credit is partly a voluntary agreement between the creditor and the debtor, and partly forced. The firm that acts as buyer simply refuses to pay the seller firm, and thereby forces it to sell the shipment on credit. If as a result the forced creditor becomes insolvent itself, it will in turn refuse payment to its own suppliers. Eventually, a veritable liquidity crisis occurs: creditors queue up before their debtors, waiting for them to kindly pay back their debts.

In view of this intolerable situation, the bank system, prompted by pity, lends a helping hand to those in the

[46]The possible increase in unemployment, which is one of the most important concomitant phenomena, will be discussed in detail on pp. 197–200.

direst straits by discounting part of their promissory notes and drafts. This is one of the distorted manifestations of Hungary's pseudo-credit system, pseudo-bank system, and pseudo-capital market. What look like genuine financial transactions simply mask the fact that it is impossible to halt production at the firms anyway, since this would spark worker protests and create production shortfalls that would lead to serious shortages, to the violation of international contracts, and so on.

Interfirm commercial credit is a natural concomitant of financial contacts and business transactions among firms. During the quantitative planning of the stabilization process, it is necessary to reckon with the existence of commercial credit. We must also put an end to its manifestation in the distorted forms of "queuing" for due payment and of the ensuing liquidity crises. We must develop the legal forms and institutions of commercial credit customary in market economies. The extortion of credit by the debtor firms should not be tolerated, but the development of voluntary credit relationships between firms should be encouraged. Discounting and passing promissory notes by endorsement should become a normal part of commercial and financial life.

This queuing of insolvent state-owned firms might also ruin some of their private suppliers who are not paid for their shipments. The state sector is inclined to assign private enterprises to the tail end of the queue of involuntary creditors. The prospects for recovering the debt are much brighter for an influential state-owned firm than for an unaided private firm. For instance, the state-owned firm might recover the debt through the intervention of the state bank sector. This is one of the areas in which the private sector is in real need of protection. In accordance with requirement No. 2 in chapter 1, it is essential to guarantee the enforcement of contracts between state-owned and private firms. If a state-owned firm becomes a selling or buying party to a contract with a private firm, then it should be obliged to comply fully with the terms of the contract. Of course, this holds true for the private firm as well.[47]

2. The issue of *wages* is the most difficult, and politically sensitive, part of the stabilization operation. We must make sure that the total amount of wages paid out by the state-owned firm sector does not exceed the limit permitted by the stabilization program. I cannot say what this limit should be as compared with the nominal wage level of the prestabilization period. It is possible that for a short time a measure of surplus purchasing power must be released, and that this will be accompanied by a wave of price increases—a transitional "corrective price-level increase" in order to absorb a portion of unspent forced

[47]For all the apparent symmetry, the situation is in fact strikingly asymmetric. If a private firm violates a contract signed with a state-owned firm, and if a suit is brought and the court metes out a one-million-forint penalty, then the private entrepreneur pays it out of his own pocket. If, however, a contract between a private firm and a state-owned firm is violated by the latter, and the penalty meted out is also one million forints, then the manager of the state-owned firm pays it not out of his own pocket but out of that of the state. Thus the state-owned firm is not afraid of these court proceedings. This is one of the most serious problems in the business ties between the two sectors. There is no ultimate and completely reassuring solution. However, the authority of the contracts could be slightly strengthened if the manager of the state-owned firm and the leaders directly responsible in the case at issue had to cover a certain part of the penalty from their own pockets.

savings and liquidate the "monetary overhang." It is also possible that this will be unnecessary; we must wait for further, extensive analysis.[48]

Once this average wage level, which must remain fixed for a while, is given, various tools may be applied to stabilize it. According to one point of view, the extension of credit to firms must be strictly tied to the adherence to wage norms. I am somewhat doubtful as to whether this will be sufficient. It seems likely that it will be necessary to apply stronger measures. Reconsidering the experiences of the past, it will be possible to single out those means of regulation that are relatively the most effective.

I do not really wish to take a position in this study on what the specific formula should be, but, for instance, a limit might be put on the total wage fund of the firm, or the wage fund might be determined as a proportion of production, or some other formula. I am aware that this will reduce the independence of the firm's managers and will render the optimal combination of factors of production more difficult. Nevertheless, if we fail to take this step, the managers of state-owned firms will continue to raise wages indiscriminately. Inevitably, we would find ourselves in the position of China a few years ago, which was that of Yugoslavia and Poland in 1989. This situation cannot be controlled indirectly. It is self-deception to expect that the manager of a state-owned firm will voluntarily keep a firm hand on wages under a system of bureaucratic state ownership.

[48]In the case of the Polish stabilization program, this kind of "corrective nominal wage increase" seemed unavoidable. It is not clear whether it will be necessary in Hungary as well.

Chapter 3 will return to the political consequences of this problem and will also discuss the role of the trade unions. At this point only economic arguments are needed. I am aware that control of runaway wages through administrative means also prejudices efficiency in several respects. But the only possibility of altering this situation lies in the replacement of state ownership with private ownership. Only private ownership can pit a natural "antagonist" against the employee who demands a wage raise; this antagonist is the owner, who pays wages out of his own pocket. This genuine and natural conflict is impossible to simulate through "pseudo-ownership reforms," and as long as state ownership remains dominant, only bureaucratic means can be applied to counter the pressure from below for wage increases.

In a mature capitalist economy a restrictive monetary policy will normally force the business sphere into freezing wages, or even into reducing them. The firm cannot obtain the demanded amount of money, and as a result it is not willing to pay its workers more. It is not certain that this mechanism works fully even in mature capitalist economies, but it has a chance. This is definitely not the case in the Hungarian economy, which is three-quarters socialist and one-quarter capitalist. Numerous examples could be quoted to prove that many state-owned firms in the direst of straits increased their employees' wages without any self-restraint. They started from the belief that it would somehow be possible to raise money for this purpose, if not for others. In the worst of cases, they did not pay their own suppliers. This is why it is impossible to avoid setting direct bureaucratic limits to the wages in the Hungarian state sector.[49] Ever since the introduction of market reform into state ownership emerged as an idea a couple of decades ago, this issue has been continuously shirked.[50] It is high time to face this bitter fact.

I emphasize again that the maintenance of wage discipline is the Achilles' heel of the stabilization operation. If we fail in this, the whole operation will come to naught.

FORMING RATIONAL PRICES

Let us start by outlining the desirable outcome. The operation will be successful if it ultimately replaces the current arbitrary and, from the economic point of view, irrational price system with a rational market price system, in which prices carry meaningful economic information. This change is subject to several conditions. Some of

[49]I hope that the above train of thought is acceptable in a direct, logical way; I do not wish to refer to authorities. I add the following just for the sake of interest.

In 1986 the Chinese government invited seven foreign experts for an exchange of views on the reform process. One of the discussions was devoted to the dangers of inflation. Three of the guests took the floor: Otmar Emminger, the former president of the West German Bundesbank, James Tobin, a Nobel Prize winning American economist who had been an economic adviser to the Kennedy administration, and myself, in this order. Both Western economists, who had spent their whole lives in capitalist conditions and who knew the ins and outs of their system's economies in both theory and practice, unhesitatingly and emphatically advised that Communist China should administratively restrain wages. I myself, being a specialist of comparative systems theory and the socialist economy, proposed the same.

The Chinese government failed to heed our advice. The wage inflation induced by runaway wages and almost insatiable investment hunger accelerated.

[50]The exceptions deserve respect. See, for example, the works of I. R. Gábor (1988) and I. R. Gábor and Gy. Kővári (1987).

these are self-evident and relatively easy to fulfill. Other conditions are fairly difficult to satisfy and contain unavoidable contradictions.

Let us begin with the self-evident part of the task. The prices of all private sector transactions should be allowed to move freely, unhampered by state intervention. This in itself is no guarantee that this "private price system" will become rational for the economy as a whole, since there are numerous units in the private sector that have contacts with the state sector either as sellers or as buyers. Consequently, the prices of the state sector will spill over to the costs and prices of the private sector. And yet the input-output flow within the private sector will be comparatively high in a number of products and services, so that for quite a number of prices the standard against which state prices could be measured will be private prices.

The rearrangement of prices in the state sector is a much tougher nut to crack. Let us begin our analysis by stating clearly what we want prices in the state sector to look like by the time the stabilization operation is completed. The goal is to develop market-clearing prices. Thus, apart from a few exceptions, *total liberalization of prices* is necessary in the state sector as well. The sooner the operation achieves this goal, the better.

The permanent exceptions are those products and services whose prices are also regulated in the most developed, mature market economies: public services, the output of natural monopolies, and so on.

While I suggest without hesitation that, as a final result of the stabilization operation, we must attain price liberalization, I can only offer *conditional* suggestions regarding the road leading to this desirable end state. The first condition we must take into account is the extent of price liberalization in the state sector already achieved by the Hungarian economy *before* the beginning of the stabilization operation. Partial price regulation and halfway price liberalization carry many risks, individually as well as in their interaction. Be they good or bad, when the surgery begins, the results of earlier partial liberalizations must be taken into account. It is clear that here a reversal in the direction of restrictions would not be advisable. (The exception would be the case in which wrong measures have been or will be instituted, which allow free prices in those areas where they are usually regulated even in developed, mature market economies.)

When considering the price system, the state of supply and the size of the reserves of essential consumer goods, energy, and raw materials must also be taken into account (see p. 164). If, as a consequence of an error by the government or bad luck, a serious shortage appears, then it will be necessary to think about whether it is worth allowing the prices of essential products and services to rise sky-high right at the outset of the stabilization. The decision may be taken to restrict prices for a short transitional period, but this restriction must be supplemented without fail by the determination to quickly increase supply—for example, by importing—and then to proceed with price liberalization. With the exception of the small sphere of permanently regulated prices, every incidence of price regulation must be regarded as a transitional evil to be ended as fast as possible. The sooner import, including private import, is freed up, and the greater the opportunity for the private sector to quickly fill the gaps left by the state sector, the sooner it will be possible to put an end to such regulation.

In the beginning of the stabilization process, the state-owned firms—unaccustomed to free prices—may have difficulties in determining their *initial* price. It is worth applying a few rules of thumb, in the full knowledge that this is only the beginning. Later, market forces can develop prices that diverge from the initial prices asked by the state firms.

As regards tradable products, a potential point of departure is the long-established principle of adjustment of domestic prices to those of the capitalist countries. First of all, we should take into account prices quoted for each product by capitalist foreign trade partners. Oversimplifying, I would say that after converting the prices with the aid of the private exchange rate, there should be no dramatic difference between foreign and domestic price systems—i.e., the price ratio of various products, for instance of electrical appliances in Vienna and Budapest, of meat in eastern Austria and western Hungary, or of cars in Munich and Budapest. Should this happen, most superfluous shopping excursions abroad would end, and without need of administrative prohibition, shopping tourism would be restricted to transactions based on comparative advantage on either side.

The realization of this concept implies the implementation of previous points in this chapter: strict uniformity of consumption tax rates and customs tariffs, and the elimination of consumers' and producers' subsidies.

During the stabilization of 1946, the initial relative

price system quoted in forints was formulated on the basis of the 1938 prices quoted in *pengő,* the Hungarian currency at the time. A similarly simple procedure is needed today. But now the basis for price formation should be the relative prices of contemporary capitalism rather than Hungarian prices of the past. For example, the firms could take present-day Austrian or West German prices as their starting point. Not that I believe that from the point of view of pure economic theory, these are exemplarily optimal prices. Nothing of the sort; these prices are also distorted by a number of factors. It also goes without saying that the demand-supply situation and the cost structure are different in Hungary. And yet these Austrian and West German prices are at least genuine prices. From among the market economies, Hungary's ties are the strongest with these countries; Hungarian businessmen and tourists in most cases compare these countries with Hungary.

Whether the point in question is the price prescribed initially by the state or the price set freely by the state-owned firm, I would suggest starting out from the following calculation: At what price could a particular product be sold or bought in Austria or in West Germany? This price should be converted into forints using the exchange rate effective at the moment of the operation. (The question of exchange rates will be discussed in the next section.) The result would be the domestic price with which the state seller enters the market at the start of the operation.

The relative prices of Hungary's private sector present a further important basis for fixing the starting prices of the operation. We have already touched on this issue in connection with the private foreign currency exchange rate. The idea, however, is far more comprehensive. Genuine market prices have already emerged in, for example, the private market for foodstuffs, the rents of privately owned flats, the real estate market, a significant part of the service sector, and other areas. It would be expedient for the state-owned firm to start out from these prices when it puts up its products on the market during the operation, precisely because these are genuine market prices and not prices cooked up artificially in an office.

Foreign prices and domestic private market prices might provide orientation in determining the *relative prices* of various products and services. These relative prices could then be used by state-owned firms when they enter the market in the course of stabilization. The *general price level* is a different question: it will depend on numerous other macroeconomic factors (supply of credit, wage level, macrosupply and macrodemand, and so on).

When the state firm makes its calculations, it takes into account the *exchange rate* determined by the state financial authorities and used by the state banking system (see the following section). The firm must also take into account positive *real interest rates* set at a rational level and exacted by the state bank sector. These rates, which should apply for at least the initial period of the operation, must be announced in advance. They can be modified later, in accordance with the real credit market situation.

But even if there are guiding posts assisting the firm in determining its price, when it finally enters the market—brought to life by the operation—it is to some degree forced to make a leap in the dark in picking its initial price.

What happens then should be determined by the free play of demand and supply. It is important to liberate all prices quickly (except for those of the permanently regulated monopolistic products). It will take a while before demand and supply reach equilibrium and a market-clearing equilibrium price can emerge. We should be mindful of the fact that in the meantime foreign trade is also going on, with most of these transactions carried out by private foreign traders. Importers turn up on the market, be they Hungarian state-owned firms, Hungarian private firms, foreign capitalist firms, or joint ventures, and they enter into competition with the domestic producer. If the initial selling price ensured high profitability, it would attract imports and would sooner or later bring the price down; in the contrary situation the processes would move in the opposite direction.

In the final analysis, liberalization leads to the development of basically *uniform* prices. It is well known that perfectly uniform prices develop only under the market structure referred to in theoretical economics as perfect competition. In the case of imperfect competition (characteristic of most branches of a developed market economy), prices are somewhat dispersed. We must, of course, anticipate this in Hungary as well. However, this is, so to speak, a "natural dispersion." What the stabilization operation must put an end to is the artificial splitting up of the price system on the basis of other criteria such as "white" versus "gray" or "black" market prices, prices diverging from market-clearing prices and dictated by the authorities versus free-market prices, prices determined by state firms versus those determined by the private sector. The tearing down of these price walls will lead to the evolution of a basically uniform price system as a result of the operation.

No one can tell how long the emergence of uniform market-clearing prices will take. We should not cherish illusions; in Hungary we cannot reckon with the emergence of an orderly and consolidated market similar to that of Frankfurt or Zurich just one year after the start of the operation. But let us not be afraid of the "anarchy" of the market. Price fluctuations are a natural part of this process, as are occasional dazzling profits or losses. Public sentiment in Hungary has already reconciled itself to the losses. But let me add that people should also be prepared to contain their accumulated sense of envy when they witness others making tremendous profits. This is the engine of adaptation. The possibility of making money hand over fist, even if only a few will succeed, might move thousands and even hundreds of thousands to take chances, to run risks, and to embark on genuine business enterprises.

Today the structure of the Hungarian economy is replete with disproportion and disharmony, but the effects of such a situation attract rather than repel the entrepreneurs, if there is genuine free enterprise (see pp. 38–50). The greater the disproportion between demand and supply, the more money can be made out of any action that restores the equilibrium of demand and supply. In a country with a truly harmonic economic structure, there is virtually no other way to earn extra income than to introduce technical innovations or important new products. But in our topsy-turvy world, those who want to make money find a real gold mine. This, however, calls for changes in the attitudes and moral judgments of the public, along the lines described in chapter 1. The economic thinking that has prevailed for decades in Hungary has prejudiced attitudes in this respect. According to its tenets, the only ethically acceptable form of income is that earned by labor, while "profiteering" or "speculation" are subject to condemnation.[51]

Another widely held judgment considers all those as dishonest who take advantage of shortages in order to make a profit. As if it were not the only sensible reaction by any seller in the market to raise the selling price in the face of shortages! Price is not a moral but an economic category. Shortages will not disappear if we ask sellers to practice self-restraint and to kindly refrain from price hikes. Preaching (or police actions) cannot make the seller renounce the utmost exploitation of his potential. Rather we should put an end to the position of superiority that he

[51]The ancient idea of establishing direct contact between the agricultural producer and the urban consumer by eliminating go-between commerce is the germ of all urban food market types. In today's Hungary, where this intermediary commerce between agricultural producers and urban consumers is undeveloped, it might well play an expedient role for the time being. Both the producer and the buyer may have the feeling that they gained. However, this can only be temporary. A lasting solution can only be achieved if an up-to-date and refined intermediary commerce is created to link producers and customers. The various purchasing and sales organizations should compete with one another. This intermediary function should be taken over to an ever greater degree by private commerce. Here we also need a genuine modern market, in which the costs and profit of the mediatory activity are brought down by competition and by the free entry of entrepreneurs.

I am convinced that this line of thought is shared by most economists. The romantic "antimarketism" and the publicity campaign against "business-minded intermediary commerce" are unjustified. Such only frighten entrepreneurs away from taking up the trading of foodstuffs and campaigns joining competition in ever greater numbers.

occupies in a sellers' market. (This problem, along with the elimination of the shortage economy in general, will be discussed in detail on pp. 171–176.)

The previous section recommended that the subsidization of loss-making state-owned firms be terminated. Let us now return to this idea again, in light of the prospective new price system. We are very much in the dark about which of the firms show a genuine loss and which run only pseudo-losses. The calculation is relatively easy in the case of the mining industry. It is virtually certain that the Hungarian uranium mine shows a grave deficit, since the cost sheet includes relatively few factors, and the value of output is also easy to define on the basis of world market prices. The same calculation, however, is practically impossible when it comes to the manufacturing industry, whose costs are affected by the spillover of a myriad of input prices, which in turn are influenced by a maze of subsidies and tax exemptions. It would not be surprising if a number of the state-owned firms that are considered loss makers today turned out to be clear of this charge after the operation. It would not be surprising either if the opposite happened, i.e., if other state-owned firms that today qualify as profitable turned out to be unprofitable once the accounts began to include realistic costs and tax burdens.

THE INTRODUCTION OF A
UNIFORM EXCHANGE RATE
AND CONVERTIBILITY

I suggest that the following very closely related tasks be performed during the operation (once the conditions to be outlined later have been fulfilled).

1. *A uniform exchange rate must be applied.*

2. *The Hungarian forint must become convertible.* The Hungarian state bank should exchange the forint freely into foreign hard currency for all Hungarian citizens and all firms and institutions.

3. *All import and export activities,* those of state-owned firms as well as the private sector, *must be liberalized.*

The first task cannot be performed by coercion, by banning private currency transactions and declaring the private exchange rate illegal. I still maintain everything stated in this connection in chapter 1: all individuals must have a right to buy and sell foreign exchange freely. Uniformity of the exchange rate will develop without administrative coercion provided currency can be bought without restriction from the state bank at a price no higher and sold at a price no lower than the private exchange rate. If the state banking sector ensures this, one can assume that the private exchange rate will be pushed somewhat lower. (And all other circumstances being equal, the exchange rate certainly will be lower than the current black market rate, which has to include compensation for the risk posed by illegality.)

To prevent the exchange rate applied by the state banking system from causing serious disproportions on the

Hungarian currency market, a *market-clearing* exchange rate is required. There is no telling exactly what that rate will be, as it will depend largely on how the other parts of the stabilization operation progress, and on how the inflation rate moves in the period up to the operation. Whatever happens, one of the main bases for deciding the rate might be today's "gray" private exchange rate. A more important gauge still might be tomorrow's "white" private exchange rate, provided the private currency market has been legalized before the operation.

All the signs indicate that one part of the operation will be the devaluation of the forint and the move toward convertibility. Before the state banking sector can ensure convertibility, numerous conditions must be fulfilled; I would like to highlight two of these.

The most important is control of the *demand* for hard currency, in which the most problematic area is the *state sector:* the demand by state-owned firms for hard currency (or the imports to be paid by convertible currency) must not be allowed to run away. Past experience is not comforting: state-owned firms under a soft budget constraint have had an almost insatiable hunger for Western imports and hard currency. Their priority has been to grab the hard currency, since there will certainly be a way to obtain the forints to pay for it later. All now depends on curbing this hunger by ensuring that the firms are rather short of forints (and a realistic, market-clearing exchange rate applies).

So the decisive factor is whether a tight monetary policy and a hard constraint on the credits granted to the state sector can be achieved, as outlined on pp. 65–80 and 140–141.

If this can be done, convertibility will be sustainable without gravely endangering the country's foreign exchange balance. If not, the problems there will start all over again, and there will be no other solution than to ration the amount of hard currency available to state-owned firms. That would have several drawbacks, but it cannot be omitted from the range of possible choices as long as the state sector remains the dominant one in the economy. There is no such danger from *private firms,* whose very nature provides them with a hard budget constraint.

The demand for hard currency by households may run away beyond the planned level if nominal wages rise faster than desired. Here, as at many other points, the strict application of wage discipline is fundamental.

Another requirement for stabilizing the exchange rate at a realistic level and ensuring convertibility is for the state to have adequate foreign currency reserves. These may be in the form of actual reserves held by the National Bank or of standby credits that can be drawn on at any time. If the state has such reserves, the appearance of excess demand for hard currency need not cause the state banking system to immediately suspend free sales of foreign currency. It can draw on the reserves instead. Of course, further measures must be taken to restore equilibrium between supply and demand, such as reducing the macrodemand expressed in domestic currency (and within it the demand of the sector whose foreign currency demand has been greater than expected), or possibly devaluing the forint again. We will return to the subject of foreign currency reserves on p. 164.

The presence of a uniform, realistic market-clearing exchange rate and of convertibility allows a comprehensive liberalization of imports (provided the conditions outlined above have been met). It then becomes admissible and desirable for all agents in the economy to conduct import activity freely. But if the conditions remain unfulfilled, only private imports can be freed without running a major risk. It is a dangerous game to give state-owned firms full freedom to import while state sector demand is still not under an effective constraint or adequate control.

All these changes might do more than help to restore the country's short-term external and internal financial equilibrium: they might also contribute to lasting expansion and quality development in production. Free importing, irrespective of whether it is done by a state-owned or private firm or a domestic or foreign importer, is indispensable to competition among sellers. This competition in turn is one of the strongest incentives to ensure that the general public is better supplied, shortage is eliminated, and technical standards are developed.

WHY SIMULTANEITY?

Quite a few of the measures described in the previous sections have already been partially implemented, or are about to be implemented. There have been frequent promises to slow down the pace of inflation. Steps are taken time and again to reduce budgetary expenditures and boost revenues. The so-called monetary restriction is proceeding at full steam, and some of the prices are already free.

The problem lies in the fact that the implementation of these changes is inconsistent and sluggish. The ambiguity that prevails in one set of measures reduces the efficiency of another set. The sum total of ten different kinds of half results is not five full successes but five full fiascos. All of the above-named measures are conditional upon one another. Stopping inflation requires a balanced budget. Balancing the budget, in turn, can be achieved only if the tax system is placed on a radically new basis. The budget cannot be balanced in the midst of inflation, since revenues are always delayed by comparison with expenses, so that inflation makes itself felt more strongly on the income side than on the expenditure side. Stopping the subsidization of loss-making firms is conditional upon the introduction of a new tax system and also upon the possibility of finding out which firms are genuine profit or loss makers through the use of market-clearing equilibrium prices. Genuine market prices cannot emerge, however, amid accelerated inflation. While the partial price adjustments do not converge to a rational system of relative prices, they themselves speed up the inflationary spiral. The list of these concentric and interdependent problems could well be extended by a dozen more examples. Taken together, they provide an economic explanation for the need to execute the operation at one stroke.

For the sake of emphasis, it is worth putting this negatively: Most of the measures beneficial as parts of the stabilization package would be dangerous and damaging if taken singly, without the other measures being implemented at the same time. For instance, total freeing of prices can cause grave damage in the absence of wage dis-

159

cipline. Full convertibility can be harmful if demand from
the state sector is not firmly controlled. The examples
could be continued. These dangers are not imagined, but
very real indeed. The stabilization measures up to now
have failed one after the other just because there was not
the right economic environment and the authorities tried
to introduce them hastily, picking up targets torn out of
their economic context.

I would like to add two further arguments to this *economic* reasoning.

The first is an economic-psychological one. If we want
to stop inflation, we must radically alter inflationary expectations. The more each employer and employee, businessman and money holder, counts on a 20 percent rise in
inflation, the more likely it is that he will adjust to this by
at least 20 percent the prices and wages asked and offered
on the market. A stabilization operation could cut the self-
fulfilling vicious circle of inflationary expectations, provided that promises to this effect come from a dependable
and respectable government.

The second argument is primarily a humanitarian one.
The population of Hungary suffers considerably as a result
of current economic ills. It is the prime obligation of political organizations, parties, and all governmental institutions to alleviate people's misery. The rehabilitation of the
economy entails serious sacrifices, but the sacrificial period should not drag on endlessly. If the only cure for a
person is to cut off his leg, it is still more humane to perform a single amputation with the necessary anesthesia
than to schedule a long-lasting operation and cut a thin
slice off every week or month. István Széchenyi, the great

nineteenth-century reform politician and one of the first Hungarian economists, used the metaphor of a tooth extraction in his volume *Credit:* "The tooth extractor or operator is cruel if he keeps pulling slowly and faintly on account of senseless soft-heartedness, and performs his job with only minor cuts and for a long time."[52]

People have every reason to become indignant at the almost weekly infringement on their well-being. We have reached a point where it is possible to call workers to strike on account of an increase in the prices of certain meat products, but where at the same time millions of households are subject to continuous but imperceptible losses amounting to a much larger sum without any protests. It is my firm belief that people would by far prefer to face a single, radical shock and the ensuing trauma if they were really convinced that the situation would improve as a result rather than to suffer the hopeless torture, the slow but steady economic deterioration and economic and social spasms we are now undergoing.

After the first presentation of my proposals in the summer of 1989 and the publication of the Hungarian edition of this book, an objection was raised. It was argued that while drastic measures are the only way to achieve a break in inflation for countries like Poland and Yugoslavia, which suffer from hyperinflation, there is no need to apply a similar strategy in a country like Hungary, where the inflation rate is much more moderate.

However, it is not the magnitude of inflation that deter-

[52]I. Széchenyi (1979), p. 214. The quote was brought to my attention by K. Szabó.

mines the fundamental choice of stabilization strategy, i.e., the choice between a gradualist approach and a surgery. In fact, a few years ago, when the Hungarian inflation rate was only in the one-digit range, I advocated a *simultaneous* radical restructuring of prices, taxation, and many other elements of the economic system in the context of fundamental political changes. A study written jointly with Ágnes Matits and published later in Hungarian (1987) stressed this viewpoint. (Excerpts of the book in English are available in Kornai [1990].) A surgical operation is needed in Hungary (and all over Eastern Europe, even in countries that have not had open inflation so far) not only because of inflation. It is needed because sequential partial measures can be harmful and do not solve the overall problems. This conviction lay at the base of the argument in the Hungarian edition, which I wrote when I was not yet familiar with the Polish program. My suggestions were based on the understanding that in a socialist economy, macroadjustment and stabilization must go along with deep, overall *systemic* changes.

Poland had an additional reason to undertake an operation as soon as possible: the intolerable acceleration of its inflation. When I learned more about the Polish program and had the opportunity to discuss it with one of its chief architects, Jeffrey Sachs of Harvard University, I felt reassured that my suggestions pointed in the right direction. Our discussions and my acquaintance with his writings (for example, Sachs and Lipton [1989a and b]) helped me to refine many important details of my proposals. In particular, the understanding of the Polish plans helped me to reconsider the Hungarian policy concerning convertibility and external debt.

162

Of course, there are similarities and differences between the Hungarian and Polish situations. Each Eastern European country in transition from socialism must face its own initial political and economic conditions. But the necessity of *simultaneous* changes in macropolicy, economic control, and property relations is common to all of them.

HUMANITARIAN AND ECONOMIC RESERVES

Society must be prepared for the operation by maintaining appropriate reserves. Four kinds of reserves are indispensable.

1. The most important is a "humanitarian" reserve, i.e., a fund that could be used to extend, under proper public supervision, an emergency grant to those in dire straits. Sooner or later everyone will have to adapt to the new market situation after the operation. Those who prove permanently unable to accommodate to the new conditions should be assisted by means of an adequate welfare policy, the details of which will be addressed in the next chapter. In other words, what I have in mind is not the permanent safety net that is a must in every humanitarian society, but extraordinary urgent relief aid to be extended in the first one or two years of the operation. This aid might also be justified for those who will be able to stand on their own feet. Indeed, it is important to lay special stress on the temporary nature of this aid. Society expects everyone who is able to stay afloat on his own to do so sooner or later. There is no need for paternalism for those

who are able to create the essential conditions for leading a normal life.

2. There must be a *reserve of goods and capacities* to assure the availability of vital consumer goods, fuel, other sources of energy, and so on. It might happen that the initial adjustment to the operation will be convulsive; in this case serious disorders can be avoided through adequate state reserves.

3. The state should dispose of enough convertible hard currency reserves to pay for extraordinary imports in case of temporary troubles. Reserves of this kind are also needed so that the state banking system can abide by its promises with regard to convertibility. Should excess demand for foreign currency appear, it should be covered in the first instance from reserves. (It is another matter to decide what means to use after the first reaction to restore equilibrium on the foreign currency market.)

4. Besides the normal amount of credit earmarked for the state and private sectors, there should be *reserve credit quotas.* These could be used to extend transitional loans to those state or private firms that face an unexpected liquidity crisis during the operation. These should be hard credits, not soft money for bailouts. If the firm manages to weather the stabilization operation with the help of such a loan, then it would have been worth the trouble. Should the firm fail, the loan would have been wasted. In this latter case the firm would have to be forbidden to reschedule the original credit or obtain a new one. The operation as a whole should result in the acceleration of the harsh natural selection process, and the transitional loans should be the last chance for those organizations that consider themselves strong enough to survive.

The financial coverage for all four kinds of reserves must be included in the plan of the operation. The stabilization operation is doomed to fail if its balance equations are more or less in equilibrium, but then it turns out later that in order to live through the crisis, it will be necessary to finance individual assistance programs, unscheduled imports, or transitional loans for firms, disrupting the precarious equilibrium. Reserves should be set aside *in advance* for such extraordinary purposes, and any remainder could still be invested. On the other hand, not a single forint or dollar above the earmarked amount could be used for such purposes.

THE STABILIZATION OPERATION IN THE INTERNATIONAL CONTEXT

The stabilization operation must rely basically on Hungarian resources and capacity. The drafters of the plan should take into account foreign assistance only to the extent that it can be counted on with absolute certainty. The plan should be pessimistic and overcautious. If foreign assistance turns out to be more than expected, the surplus can always be put to good use. At the same time, I am convinced that precisely those changes described in chapter 1, and also the stabilization operation itself, will considerably widen the scope for foreign assistance. Let us examine the most important tasks in this context.

1. Both the current and the new postelection governments should reshape in a calm manner Hungary's ties with the Comecon countries. The longer-term aims are complex. On the one hand, Hungary should reduce its

dependence on both the export and the import sides. On the other hand, the country needs to promote a more advantageous structure of its foreign trade.

The most important long-term drawback of Hungary's export ties with the Comecon countries is the low level of quality standards in these markets. Remarkably, this lack of high standards and of ambitious demands concerning the quality of goods is precisely what makes these commercial ties so attractive for state-owned firms and makes them stick to these markets. It is relatively easy to sell products in these markets that would be unacceptable in hard currency markets. This is one more reason for the need to coolly but resolutely shift Hungary's sphere of interest to markets that insist on higher-quality goods. In the meantime it is most important that the Hungarian government take special care to maintain business continuity even in the wake of political change. Once signed, the business contract must not be violated unilaterally; this is the basic law of honest trading. Hungary's reliability must in no way be undermined. The unilateral cancellation of economic agreements is acceptable only under emergency conditions, and such a move must always be approved by Parliament.

2. Regarding Hungary's ties with the Western economies, a few words are in order concerning the problems of private foreign capital—all the more so since the attitude of Western governments and the international organizations toward Hungary is usually given disproportionate emphasis in public debates. To be sure, their behavior matters a good deal to Hungary, but I maintain that the attitude of Western businessmen, entrepreneurs, and pri-

vate firm managers is of even greater significance. There is no "Capitalist International," and the capitalists of the world have not united. They do not dance to the piping of some world center, be it Washington, Bonn, or Tokyo. Their actions are coordinated by the invisible hand of the market, through the method of trial and error. They do listen to government statements, but often they pay much closer attention to their fellow businessmen relating their Hungarian experiences in a common club. The bitter story of one disappointed acquaintance about the many bureaucratic obstacles he had to face in Hungary is enough to spoil a hundred government guarantees. A socioeconomic system cannot have two faces: an ugly one toward its own citizens and a charming one toward the outside world. We cannot keep building Potemkin villages: while Budapest's downtown is graced with elegantly furnished Western-style banks, it remains impossible for callers from provincial towns to reach the capital by phone, and clients in provincial towns have to queue up for hours just to accomplish a basic banking transaction.

Hungary's ties with the Western business world will improve and become organic to the degree that the economic standards, culture, and liberties of Hungary's private sector develop. A sensible, sober-minded Western capitalist who cannot easily be cheated has no confidence in the *exceptional* conditions granted to him: special tax exemptions, special convertibility terms, and special customs duties applicable to foreigners only. He will trust, however, those conditions granted to every Hungarian citizen without condescension. If, pursuant to chapter 1, an enterprising Hungarian citizen can conduct business without having to endure the torture of licensing, then a foreign citizen will also embark in his business with much greater calm. If the Hungarian citizen is levied taxes that are uniform, transparent, and flat, then the foreign entrepreneur will not fear an imminent tax progression. The list could well be extended. In this area there is also need for a continuous, gradual, and organic development. It is desirable that as many of these changes as possible be realized before the start of the operation.

In my view the operation itself could further increase the confidence of Western businessmen. They would find it reassuring to see order and stability gain the upper hand over inflation, the budget deficit, the distorted prices, and an inscrutable tax system.

3. The previous statements are, of course, not meant to play down the importance of the assistance Hungary could obtain from Western governments and international financial institutions. Without going into details here, I wish to make just one comment. The stabilization operation is the very best occasion for mobilizing a considerable part of Western assistance. There are many people in the Western political and economic world who feel that they were already burned by the experience of their unbridled lending in the 1970s, when their loans melted away in the hands of borrowing governments. In the case of Hungary, the governments in power have since the 1970s presented new reform schemes each year, while the debts continued to mount and economic ills worsened.

This time a unique opportunity presents itself. There is a great chance that Hungary will have a freely elected Parliament and a new government that will enjoy its support. Let us add that, in the spirit of this book, this new government has the chance to present a clear-cut stabilization program. Foreign governments could well be won over to this cause, and their support could take various forms: we could receive aid, extraordinary loans under better than average conditions, and perhaps a more considerate treatment of our existing debts as well. In my opinion foreign governments and international organizations are more inclined to back an operation that is scheduled to be enacted in the foreseeable future, within one or two years, than to respond to some oblique promises relating to the distant future.

4. In its program the new government should pledge its word to the Hungarian nation to renegotiate the country's debts with its creditors, but it should abstain from announcing a rescheduling in the conventional sense of the term. Such a move would only undermine Hungary's authority in the financial world. The country may be able to avoid rescheduling under the pressure of an emergency situation.

This, however, does not mean that the country must acquiesce blindly and unquestioningly to the size of the debt-service burden to be borne by the present generation of Hungarian citizens. The nation as a whole has already suffered too much, and may not be able to heed new calls for patience and self-restraint over the decades to come. Nor can it be expected to accept further suffering in exchange for promises of a better world that will come true sometime in the distant future, perhaps in the year 2010 or 2050. The debt burden borne by the Hungarian people must be eased now, within the next couple of years.

This is a controversial problem among Western economists and economic policymakers as well, as there are several countries in the world struggling to pay off their debts. The leaders of the national central banks behave in a very similar way concerning these issues, irrespective of whether the debtor is a socialist or a capitalist country. Their main criterion is a negative one: "Take care not to annoy the creditor banks!" A pat on the back at the club of international bankers is a great compliment, enough to offset grumbling back home. In addition, those at the political helm are usually ignorant of international financial matters and trust their own bankers unreservedly. If their own bankers frighten them by exclaiming: "It will have a bad end if we do not pay!" they will react with due attention and will readily opt for forcing people to further tighten their belts.

The debtor is at the mercy of his creditor, but the creditor is exposed to the debtor as well. Parallel to the announcement of its stabilization program, the new government of Hungary should also pledge its determination to reduce the debt service burden. There is no need to act with precipitation, and the government should not under any circumstances violate one single credit contract arbitrarily. But there must be separate negotiations with each group of creditors: the so-called Paris Club of Western creditors, the various governments, international financial institutions, Eastern European trading and financial partners, and so on. An attempt must be made to persuade each group of creditors, calmly but emphatically, that Hungary cannot and will not repay its debts according to the original schedule. The country needs a judicious renegotiation of its obligations. It is necessary to conclude as many of these revisions as possible already during the period leading up to the operation. Later the operation itself will provide occasion for continued negotiations.

During the negotiations, and presumably afterward, our short-term interest-payment obligations will have to be met in full. However, there are chances of reducing our medium- and long-term obligations. Several countries have negotiated successfully to do so in the last few years. This may somewhat impair Hungary's published credit ratings for the time being, but I agree with those who say this drawback is worth accepting. For one thing, Hungary even then will still be among the countries with a better credit rating. For another (and this is the decisive argument), the restructuring of the debt is vital to ensure that the stabilization operation does not place almost intolerable burdens on the public.

ELIMINATION OF THE
SHORTAGE ECONOMY

Inflation and shortage coexist in Hungary today.[53] In this section I suggest how to eliminate shortage, closely interlinked with inflation, in the context of the stabilization operation. This course of action is also related to the evolution of private enterprise described in chapter 1.

The shortage syndrome is a complex phenomenon; its

---

[53]G. W. Kolodko and W. W. McMahon (1987) called this phenomenon "shortageflation," a term coined after "stagflation," which refers to the simultaneous occurrence of stagnation and inflation.

emergence is affected by several factors. It is a problem at both the micro- and macrolevels. The socialist system's property relations and coordination mechanism, as well as its financial and price system, are among the causes. There is a chance to eliminate the shortage economy in Hungary, because past developments took place and future changes will occur in all these dimensions simultaneously.

One cannot expect shortage to disappear without trace after the operation. For quite some time we will have a market whose mechanism operates with greater friction and weaker adaptive features than those of older, well-tried markets. But one can expect the main factors pointing to the chronic, general shortage economy to be basically eliminated by the social transformation described in chapter 1 and the stabilization operation described in this chapter.

Since we have already mentioned all the conditions of eliminating the shortage economy, suffice it to give here a concise list.

1. In the course of the stabilization operation, macrodemand and macrosupply must be equilibrated. Should we manage to accomplish this during the operation and also to maintain this new equilibrium, then we will have eliminated one of the fundamental causes of shortage: excess demand at the macrolevel.

I must emphatically warn the reader that once demand runs away again, it is likely to produce inflationary pressure as well as an inducement for the reproduction of shortage. More precisely, if the government prevents prices from rising so as to counteract excess demand, repressed inflation will inevitably occur, along with shortage.

This is a real danger. If the stabilization operation falls through, or if macrodemand runs away again in the post-operation years, then we have every reason to expect wide-ranging calls for curbing price increases. Various groups will exert increasing political pressure in favor of price ceilings and the introduction of a price freeze, which will in turn lead to the rebirth of repressed inflation, itself one of the generators of shortage.

This is another argument for the need to create genuine equilibrium at the macroeconomic level during the operation. If an error is committed, it should be on the side of excess supply rather than excess demand.

2. I consider it necessary to highlight, as a separate point, the need to keep a tight hold on the state sector's demand. It is hopeless to expect hard budget constraints to prevail at the micro level in state-owned firms given the existing dominance of the state sector. In this context the term "hard budget constraint" means that the firm would voluntarily restrain its expenses as a result of its own internal motivation. But the development of a genuine profit incentive in the state-owned firm is quite unlikely. The propensity toward investment hunger and wage drift is bound to recur time and again. This is why I propose that the state sector's propensity toward spending be limited from outside, and from above.

The methods for this task have not been developed yet, but the chances of their emergence are improving. The situation was different earlier, when all the regulative powers were held by the top state bureaucracy, which was one soul, one body with state-owned firms. This almighty bureaucracy displayed a high propensity to spend at every level of the hierarchy. But now an *independent counter-*

force might emerge in the form of a multiparty Parliament. Not being a part of the bureaucracy, this legislative body will in fact be *superior* to it; as the repository of the nation's will, it will be empowered to set limits to expenditures. I hope that a legislature acting independently of the bureaucracy, or more precisely as its superior, will be able to impose restrictions on state-owned firms' propensity to spend. Accordingly, this legislature should be able to set an *economy-wide* hard budget constraint on the state sector. If it manages to do this, then it will stop one of the basic mechanisms in the reproduction of shortage. If it fails, shortage is bound to reappear.

3. One of the basic methods of eliminating the shortage economy is the expansion of the private sector. This role has already been partially fulfilled by the private sector: several kinds of demand that the state sector is unable to meet are satisfied by formal and informal private activity. The fact that shortage has been much less characteristic of Hungary than of many other socialist countries can be ascribed to, among other things, the scope of the second economy, which partly filled in the gaps left by the first economy.

The budget constraint of the private sector is hard: its spending is strictly restrained by the simple fact that the private owner has to pay from his own pocket. For this reason there is no danger that the private sector's demand will run away. Consequently, there is no intrinsic mechanism reproducing excess demand, as is the case in the state sector.

In the spirit of what has been said on pp. 34–57 and 80–93, the private sector will, I hope, prosper. It is most desirable that the public understand the logic of operation of private initiative and the market under these circumstances. It is precisely shortage that attracts the entrepreneur like a magnet, provided he is allowed to profit from the shortage situation. An overstocked market cannot offer a sizable profit. But once solvent demand appears where supply is not sufficient, mobile capital will rush in to capture any business prospective. This kind of flexibility, initiative, ability to quickly recognize and exploit opportunities, and freedom of entry and competition can together pave the way toward mastery of the thousands of microshortages.

The free entry of private enterprise into all fields of production and trade, inclusive of free private imports, can bring about a market regime that is commonly known as a buyers' market, that is, a situation in which sellers compete for the buyer.[54]

4. The freedom and flexibility of prices is a requirement related to all three points above. It is indispensable for maintaining macroequilibrium between demand and supply, and also for ensuring the quick adjustment between demand and supply at the microlevel. Free prices should in general gain the upper hand in the wake of the stabilization operation.

In the Introduction I drew a distinction between the tasks to be executed at one stroke and those that can be carried out only gradually. The elimination of the short-

[54]Under the conditions of capitalism, this emerges primarily in the market structure of so-called imperfect competition. Sellers try to win over buyers from competitors by providing better-quality, polite service and faster delivery. See the works of T. Scitovsky (1971) and E. Domar (1987).

175

age economy requires the combination of the two types of tasks. The stabilization operation will call into existence some of the conditions necessary for eliminating shortage (macroequilibrium, extensive liberalization of prices), but there are further conditions that complete the list of requirements. These are the long-term tasks, namely those related to the healthy development of the private sector, and to the continued and effective control of the state sector's demand.

OPERATION AND RECOVERY

Having surveyed the main components of the stabilization operation, here are a few final comments.

No country has ever performed the operation proposed in this book. The Soviet Union managed to terminate or radically slow down inflation after the two world wars. However, the social and, above all, political conditions surrounding the Soviet program were radically different from the current situation in Hungary.

Quite a number of large-scale stabilization operations were performed in the capitalist world after World War II. In 1946 Hungary was on the borderline between East and West when it terminated the fastest-growing hyperinflation in world history. Although some elements of the ensuing socialist system were already present (the Communist party's advance toward power, the presence of the Soviet army), the economy on the whole still operated on the basis of private ownership. Stabilization pooled the energies of all the political parties that promoted reconstruction at the time, and was supported by both private capital and organized labor.

The oft-cited West German reform of 1948 was a great success, and again it was an *operation* in the strictest sense: the changes implemented at one stroke managed to simultaneously introduce a stable currency and an almost complete liberalization of the economy. However, this was done in a fundamentally private economy. A few huge monopolistic organizations were broken up, but property relations were left untouched. Erhard (widely credited with being the architect of the West German social market economy) and his advisers had plenty of factors to consider, but they were not faced with the task of producing artificial private owners as if in a laboratory. After all, they were surrounded by flesh-and-blood private owners.

An analysis of the experiences of other radical stabilization operations (such as those of Israel or Bolivia) falls beyond the scope of the present study. Suffice it to say that although these operations were performed in seriously ill economies, and notwithstanding that the public sector in those countries was already much larger than in Erhard's Germany, the economies of Israel and Bolivia were also basically private economies.

Hungary and Poland are the first countries to approach two major tasks simultaneously, namely the transition of the economy toward the dominance of the private sector, and fundamental macroadaptation and stabilization. This combination of tasks is extremely difficult.

The steadfast and rapid implementation of the operation might give people the impression that the period of spasms and convulsions will be over within the foreseeable

177

future. Those who have undergone a serious disease or have seen the sufferings of a loved one know well the state of mind that makes the patient turn to the doctor and declare: "I can stand this no longer. Come what may, put me out of my misery. I would risk the operation, but do something with me." I feel that the Hungarian population is approaching a point where it cannot tolerate further suffering. People are fed up with the perpetual tinkering and concomitant sense of uncertainty. I believe they are ready to take the risks of a radical operation. And for all the temporary trauma and troubles it would cause, the operation at least holds out the promise of genuine order and calm.

3

Tasks of the Economic Transition from a Political Viewpoint

THE POPULARITY OF THE PROGRAM

How popular is the program of transition outlined in the previous chapters? Of course, it is impossible to please everyone in all respects. My program is not populist. But before dealing with the points to which opposition is to be expected, I will highlight those elements that can be seen as potentially popular. However, even these elements will not be received favorably by all; their attractive force will depend on the ethical and political views and economic interests of the citizens.

1. The concept outlined in this book will attract truly *liberal* people.[55] Individual freedom is not an exclusive

[55]The term "liberal" (as opposed to "conservative") has a special meaning in political language in the United States. The book uses the word "liberal" in the European political and intellectual tradition. Its meaning becomes clear in the next few sentences, and is also used in the same sense in chapter 1.

value; for most Hungarians, there are other values that count for a great deal, such as the material welfare of society, equality, social justice, and the primacy of national interest over individual interest. These values are often complementary to one another, but they might clash as well. The developmental path outlined here attracts those who see individual autonomy and the sovereignty of the citizen as equal to or higher in rank than other values. These are the people who reject the subjection of the individual to the interests of the state and to the collective interests ordered by movements, parties, or leaders.

In the paragraph above we could replace the word "individual" with "family." The draft program makes no distinction between individual, taken in a literal sense, and family, which is the smallest community of individuals. It demands autonomy and sovereignty for the family; it seeks to entrust the family with the largest possible degree of economic decision-making.

"Freedom" has become a fashionable word in Hungary these days. My study aims at giving a more concrete meaning to this word in the economic sphere. Each and every individual and family should be free to dispose of their labor power, products, free time, money, and wealth. At long last, the state should leave the individual and the family alone; it should intervene only in cases when other individuals or families need protection from those who really abuse their freedom.

2. I am convinced that the ideas raised in this book will appeal to those who are willing to embark boldly on an *enterprise* (in the sense described in this study), who are ready to take risks and to invest their money and wealth.

I cannot go along with those who see only one proper way of human behavior. Far be it from me to censure disciplined employees, those who work out their time properly, follow the directives of their supervisors, then go home after work and spend the remainder of the day relaxing or taking care of family affairs. The majority of people fall in this category. I also understand that there are meditative people who reflect upon the world and make grumbling remarks. These individuals might also play a beneficial, thought-provoking role. And finally there are those who, as a result of an unfavorable coincidence of circumstances, are unable to be particularly active even though they possess the necessary internal motivations (this group will be discussed separately).

While stressing again that there is no trace of criticism in my thoughts toward the above forms of behavior, I wish to make it quite clear that my program does not rely on these kinds of people. Here we must return to Adam Smith. People who are prepared to undertake additional tasks for their own sake and that of their families, and earn extra money, simultaneously benefit the community. National income and national wealth are not elevated collectivist categories, nor mysterious economic statistical notions. By seeking additional income, you increase national income. Accumulate more wealth for yourself, and you boost the wealth of the nation. Build a house for yourself, and you add to the nation's housing stock. Collect a thousand dollars in your drawer, and you contribute to the nation's hard currency stock. National welfare is but the sum total of individual welfares.

People must alter their way of thinking. Enrichment

has long been considered something shameful. A fallacy has reached the marrow of people's bones: if someone gets more, then it is because he took it away from others. Those who do well grind down the others, and it is a disgrace that the rich do not dole out their wealth immediately. If they are not willing to do this voluntarily, then their wealth must be taken away from them.

The country is now gripped by a grave economic crisis. Respect should go not to those who moan the loudest, but to those who stop whining and, instead of going begging for help from office to office, set about improving *their own* financial status. Instead of complaining, people should work overtime, grow fruit or vegetables in their gardens, invest in their own enterprises, team up with others and set up firms, bring in some kind of product from abroad that is much in demand at home and sell it, and so on. There are thousands of opportunities open to all. The old adage "God helps those who help themselves" has never been more appropriate. State assistance should go to those who are really unable to help themselves. But those who have the ability but still fail to do so out of passivity, indolence, or cowardice deserve neither censure nor pity. These people are the victims of socialism in that it has sapped them of personal initiative in the past decades. Change will not come primarily as the result of a new kind of moral education, although that too is needed. Public attitudes will be changed by social changes themselves. People will sooner or later realize that everyone must carve out his own fortune.

This is an organic complement to point 1. The concept raised in this book is attractive to those who claim individual (or family) autonomy, and to those who want to make use of this autonomy. It appeals to those who are able and willing to launch their own initiative, activity, and enterprise.

3. The concept might be attractive to those who have their own *property* or wish to acquire it. Here I have in mind the widest spectrum of property, ranging from the smallest units (a small garden or a modest amount of private saving) to small- and medium-size units (family house, private shop or workshop) to all larger units. But whatever the size of this property, the owner must be protected from arbitrary state conduct.

In a system of healthy political pluralism, there emerge parties and associations that focus the interests on specific groups of owners. Some of these specialize, exclusively or primarily, in protecting small-scale farmers, while others support the urban lower-middle classes or large-scale entrepreneurs. There may certainly be political forces with broader programs, able to "reach across" subgroups of owners. The present book is not meant to advise these organizations. All political forces that consider the safety and free development of private property a priority can identify themselves with the ideas proposed here.

The aim of this study is not only to encourage private accumulation but also to propose a policy that could clear the obstacles in its path. To cite an example from agriculture: I do not propose the reestablishment by state regulations of the Kulak,[56] so ruthlessly eliminated in an earlier

[56] *Kulak* is the Russian word for well-to-do farmer.

period. Instead of proposing a kind of artificial "re-Kulakization," I argue for a process of rural embourgeoisement. We ought to be pleased to witness the emergence through organic development of capital-intensive farms well equipped with modern technical equipment, which, like Danish, West German, and American farms, could assume an ever greater share in agricultural production using decreasing amounts of labor.[57]

Apart from agriculture, the transition route might also

[57]As in earlier cases, here again I do not consider references to Western examples apt. It is not enough to say, "Well, the small-scale farmers are subsidized by the state even in America and in several Western European countries." This is a rather controversial issue; there are many people who consider this a deficiency rather than a virtue of the economic policy in Western countries. It is just possible that some of the parliamentary deputies there support subsidization to attract more votes. It is conceivable that the same consideration would motivate parliamentary deputies in Hungary as well. But since I do not offer myself as a candidate for a seat in Parliament, I can feel free to speak my mind.

What I have said about the humanitarian requirements of transition applies here as well. The modernization of Hungary's agriculture must take place under humane circumstances. If, for example, a new type of small farm is about to secede from the agricultural cooperatives, it may be justified to extend nonrecurrent financial support, or an extraordinary long-term credit as an "initial momentum." This could help keep the new farm afloat.

But at a later stage private agricultural farms should be exposed to the same tough market conditions in which the rest of the private sector operates. These farms should not be granted permanent state subsidies. They should have access to short-, medium-, and long-term credits, but the terms of these credits should not be softer than those applied in the other spheres of the private sector.

It might well be that a small firm is more productive over a longer period than an inefficient cooperative. In this case the former can survive. But the time may come when a small, poorly equipped farm falls behind modern small- and medium-size farms, and then it might lose ground if not assisted by government intervention. In such a case the smallholder should be granted a *temporary* accommodation assistance until he and his family find a new form of life better suited to them. But we must not accept a situation in which a stratum of society with the ability to work, or any particular kind of economic form, can survive only through the support of the state budget.

attract those who are willing to sacrifice and save for the sake of solid enrichment. I do not want to encourage business adventurists to scrape together whatever they can and make off with it. The economic policy proposed here seeks to give material, moral, and legal guarantees to those who save from year to year, invest their money in their own enterprise, and make it grow from a small firm into a medium-size, and later on into a large-size or even mammoth, firm.

Lenin wrote that production on a small scale creates capitalism day by day and hour by hour, and he was right. Those who are frightened by this prospect obviously cannot go along with the development outlined in this program, since they want to keep even the most prosperous small-scale producer from outgrowing small-scale production. These people take the stance that it is all right to own a small plot or a workshop. If owners do well, it is all right for them to spend their money on luxury tours or to build a flashy summer house. But they must be prevented by means of bureaucratic intervention from growing from a small-scale producer into a genuine capitalist. The present study utterly rejects this line of thought. It seeks to establish the natural conditions necessary for the accumulation of private capital. The program appeals to those who see this as a reassuring opportunity.

4. The stabilization operation holds out the prospect of *stopping inflation.* In my opinion this aspect will attract millions, save a narrow group of exploiters of the inflationary process. Just consider the amount of political support to be gained by political groups if they promised to stop inflation, assumed full responsibility for carrying out

the operation, and *kept their word.* There are many who would be more than willing to make sacrifices just to stop inflation.

It is regrettable that in the midst of the countless price rises, no one has yet made such a promise. This is one of the reasons why people see the situation as hopeless. Today they are angry because price increases are announced officially every week, and they become angrier the next day because prices continue to rise without any official announcement. In fact, if we consider the average of the national economy, the problem is not as serious in terms of *real* consumption as the popular mood would suggest. There are wide social strata in which price rises are compensated, or sometimes even exceeded, by increases in nominal wages. And still, everyone becomes outraged at the constant price increases. This is why a definite and unambiguous stabilization program could become fairly popular, even if its promoters announce openly and in advance that it will result in a great shock and a nonrecurrent major price increase. But it cannot be emphasized enough that such a stabilization program will remain popular only if its promoters keep their promise.

5. The promise to *eliminate the shortage economy* is one of the attractive points of the program. As in the case of inflation, it is also regrettable that in fact no political current or party program has assumed this obligation. And yet this is one of the gravest complaints of the population: villagers and townsfolk, young and old, poor and rich, all suffer from shortage, queuing, and the sense of being at the mercy of the seller. Shortages worry consumers and constantly intrude upon the work of producers. In former

times, for those Hungarians who crossed the Hungarian-Austrian border, one of the first great experiences was the immediate realization that, for a price, everything was available in Austria. This was one of the most perceptible differences between the two systems. The elimination of shortage could bring about a similarly perceptible change: it could prove to Hungarian citizens that the system had undergone a genuine change and that at long last Hungarians could also enjoy the advantages of a buyers' market.

6. The economic policy outlined here will attract all those who are not indifferent to the fate of the *state's money,* and who are fed up with its being squandered. These people demand that all officials who have state money at their discretion should be subject to a tough, public political supervision.

7. The program will be neither highly attractive nor excessively alarming to those who have an affinity for the *principle of state ownership.* We are talking not only about the managers of state-owned firms but also about those who have long been and still are hearty supporters of socialist principles, and who see an intrinsic value in the fact that the means of production are not privately owned. The economic policy proposed here cautions against the offensive and irresponsible liquidation of state ownership. It warns against carrying out the reverse action as precipitously and with a similar irresponsibility as the radical elimination of private property. This program wishes to create genuine, not fake, rivalry between sectors. The role of the private sector should increase in direct ratio to its ability to prove its superiority to bureaucratic state ownership. Private entrepreneurs should have the opportunity

to buy certain units of the state sector, but only at a pace they can afford, relying on their own funds and on the amount of credit they are able to obtain (offering their own wealth as collateral).

The program blocks neither the development of institutional ownership by genuinely autonomous institutions nor that of genuine cooperative ownership.

All this can be accomplished as a result of an organic development. We will have to wait many years before the share of state ownership remaining after organic embourgeoisement becomes clear. By all accounts, this share should be small enough to force the state sector's behavior to conform to that of the private sector, which, of course, has a hard budget constraint, is genuinely market oriented, and pursues a steadfast business policy—and not the other way around.

For those who remain convinced of the viability of the state sector, this change in the state sector is a prospect that should prompt them to active work rather than to furious resistance. By any account, this program is more attractive than those that want to eliminate state ownership in one stroke.

8. The proposed policy calls for a halt to the *dissipation and squandering of state resources and property,* no matter what the pretext might be. This is a phenomenon that annoys and even scandalizes people. For decades slogans propagated the notion that the wealth of the state was the wealth of the people. This is only a half truth. It did not, and in fact could not, prove to be true inasmuch as the ten million citizens of this country obviously could not them-

selves control the complex production process. As this study has already stated, state property belongs to everyone and to no one.

However, the slogan was right in that the labor and the sacrifices of this country's population were embodied in the state's wealth. People have the right to know the destiny of this great treasure. The program proposed here demands that all kinds of sales be carried out in the limelight of publicity and under fair business conditions. This is a popular idea that might gain supporters for the program.

9. State wealth must not be sold to foreign countries at rock-bottom prices, as if at a liquidation sale. Here again we need an enlightened *national* policy rather than myopic isolationism, xenophobia, or anti-Western biases. It can be extremely beneficial if foreign businessmen purchase firms in Hungary, establish offices and shops, or join Hungarian enterprises, provided that these are useful to the Hungarian people. The many opening ceremonies of new Hungarian-Western joint ventures, with all the media coverage and exchanges of documents and champagne toasts, do not constitute an index of success. Instead, one would like to see concrete analyses that prove objectively that these transactions are really beneficial for Hungary.

We must establish legal limits that will prevent the all-out intrusion of foreign capital. Instead of spoiling the interest of foreign capital through bureaucratic bans, we should indicate as clearly and as frankly as possible the limits to our welcome and our conceptions of excess and trespassing.

This kind of national policy—assertive yet free of any trace of chauvinism—may well exert a strong attractive force.

Another comment concerning the national character of the program is worthwhile. The present study has repeatedly called attention to the fact that there is no need to imitate slavishly the institutions of the Western business world. This warning is not rooted in the belief that Hungary should sooner or later devise a tricolored stock exchange instead of incorporating the experiences of the New York, Zurich, and Tokyo exchanges. My unfashionable warning is based on the conviction that there are a number of institutions that can evolve soundly only as the result of an organic historical development.

A variety of institutions were unable to take root during the past decades because they were artificial and ill-conceived delusions imposed on society. The new stage in Hungary's historical development will give natural birth to the various organizational forms, legal institutions, and social manners of the market and of economic management and the business world. These will obviously be affected by foreign examples and contacts with Western partners. Let us learn from them as much as we can, but with dignity. It is not a number one priority to make foreign bankers or industrialists grant us their seal of approval; quite often they do this on superficial impressions anyway. Good marks must be earned at home.

10. Finally, the policy outlined in this study may have yet another attraction: it creates *order* out of chaos. The vast majority of Hungarian citizens feel that their country

now lives in a state of upheaval, disorganization, and disorder. Rules come and go on a daily basis. They say one thing today, tomorrow its opposite. Contradictory measures are implemented, and the economic manager or the individual may well feel free to choose which of them to obey and which to violate. Law has no authority. People have no special qualms about breaking a rule; at best they are put out if they are caught.

Meanwhile, people associate "order" with frightful notions: tanks, jailings, and the existential ruin of outspoken people come to their mind. Many see the terms "pro-order" and "re-Stalinizer" as synonyms. According to the oft-quoted bitter saying of Sándor Szalai, a noted Hungarian social democratic sociologist, we have only two choices: either the barracks or the brothel. Those who do not like barrack-room discipline must put up with the anarchy of the brothel.

But I see a third alternative. Hungary needs order, but not of the barrack type. The proposed policy wants to outline how this kind of order could be achieved. Let us put an end to the suspense created by inflation; let us rid the country of the situation in which it is impossible to calculate as prices change overnight. There should be stable laws to guarantee individual autonomy, private property, and the security of savings and investment. The state budget should be balanced. The state's practice of unbridled spending and of printing money to cover expenditures must be stopped.

Consequently, this is a pro-order program—and that might be one of the main sources of its attraction.

SOURCES OF TENSION

I would not like to raise false hopes. This program both attracts and repels; it arouses sympathy and stirs up resistance. The positions taken for and against it do not fall into a simplified Marxist pattern in which the interests of one class are defended and those of another are attacked. Using the term "class" in the Marxist sense, various members of one and the same class may react to the proposed policy in several different ways. In fact, to go further, even one individual may react to the program in an ambivalent way. Although in my opinion the policy outlined in this study forms an integral whole, many will feel they are ready to accept some of its points while rejecting others. One can expect a variety of tensions, of which I would like to mention only a few.

(a) *The wages of employees in the state sector.* An attempt to apply the proposed economic policy in the face of active resistance from employees in the state sector would result in catastrophe. In fact, it would be impossible. In this respect, it is worth reflecting on some examples from abroad.

One such example is a comparison between postwar German and British development. In victorious Britain the Labour party came to power and nationalized several industries. There was exceptional growth in the power of the trade unions. The battle for redistribution arrived to stay. The unions sought to secure a greater share for the organized workers by staging major strikes. On more than one occasion relatively small groups of workers with a key role in production were able to paralyze entire industries.

Although Britain's economic growth did not cease and did not attain crisis proportions, progress was quite sluggish and fell behind that of Britain's competitors.

The situation developed differently in defeated West Germany. During the stabilization operation, power was held by a liberal-conservative coalition that later governed alternately with a liberal–social democratic coalition; for a short time, there was a grand coalition. But the constant factor throughout was the constructive cooperation of the trade unions with the state and the private sector. In other words, to use the pejorative Bolshevik characterization, there was "class peace." All three main actors in the severely damaged West German economy—the sector in the hands of private owners (large-, medium-, and small-scale), the state bureaucracy, and employees represented by unions—realized that bickering over redistribution would be a suicidal course. To continue an image used earlier in the study, the main thing is to have a larger and larger piece of bread in our hands, not to squabble over the piece we have.

I would not want to trace back to a single factor the great difference in development that arose between post-war Britain and West Germany in the latter's favor. But it does seem as if the differences just noted were among the major, and perhaps the most important, explanatory factors.

Let us take an example closer to home: Poland. For the past ten to fifteen years, until recently, when the government of national unity was set up, there was war between employees and the state as employer. It was a struggle unique in history, since the fight for democratic liberties on the Solidarity side was bound up with "regular" labor union activity (i.e., the strike movement striving to raise nominal wages). It was at once a heroic espousal of parliamentary democracy and the preparation of economic disaster. This struggle most resembled a hunger strike, in which a political hero would sooner die than abandon his principles, except that millions of people are usually ready to make such heroic gestures only for a short transitional period. After that they want to eat their fill not once but every day. They want bread and meat, and what is more, they want a quiet, comfortable life. The material conditions for such an existence were undermined by constant work stoppages. The recent changes in Poland may have created the conditions for the kind of coalition in which there can be agreement among the main actors in the economy: the bureaucracy, the managers of the state sector, and the private sector, along with employees in both the state and private sectors.

And now let us turn from the foreign examples to the situation in Hungary. What prospects does the economic policy outlined in the study present to employees in the state sector? A great deal of what was listed in the ten points of the last section could be attractive to them as well, for most of it is not "class dependent." For example, it could be that a factory worker with no intention of starting an enterprise himself would gladly see the private peasant farm of his brother back in the village prosper or his son join a private enterprise in the town. He too is a citizen beset by the bureaucracy's multitudinous restrictions, and the proposed program's liberalism and defense of civic rights will make his life easier.

But I do not want to obscure the real dilemma. As pp. 65 and 142–145 have plainly declared, I am advocating *strict wage discipline.* This entails freezing wages in the state sector during the stabilization operation or allowing them to rise only to a modest extent. Implementation of the actual stabilization plan will show how large that raise can be, if there can be one at all; I cannot attach a figure to it. But the nominal wage level laid down in the stabilization operation must be imposed with an iron hand. If the reins are dropped here, all will be lost, and everything will go back to square one: runaway wages will be followed by runaway prices; if the prices are held down in response to demagogic demands, there will be shortage on a mass scale; and so on. We will be back where we were before the operation. The great upheaval will have been fruitless; and after that it will be much, much harder or simply impossible to undertake another operation.

It may not be possible to persuade state employees to agree in advance to accept this self-denying wage discipline. An effort must be made to convince them that this is essential, if the nation is to escape economic catastrophe. Ultimately, when the operation is complete, they too will be among the beneficiaries of the changes. This is not a "zero-sum game" where one side's gains equal the other's losses. Here everyone can be a winner. The West German workers of today have gained more than their fellows in Britain. When the economy finally recovers, production grows, inflation falls, prices can be trusted, earned forints stop melting away in their pockets, and the purchasing power of their savings remains steady, the workers will benefit as well.

195

Employees have been robbed of the right to strike for decades, and they are now beginning to realize what a massive weapon they hold. I appreciate that it is not easy to resist the temptation of using that power.

Rivalry has broken out in the trade union movement. Anyone observing the situation today as a historian or political sociologist finds the conduct of many union officials easy to explain. Up until now they have been accused of complicity with the party in power and the state bureaucracy, and of acting as their "transmission belts." Many may now feel this is the moment to show that this is no longer the case. The move is popular with the workers and entails no risk; no one these days gets whisked away by the secret police for instigating a strike.

I am not preaching that the unions must lay down their arms. Trade union officials should be on guard against real injuries to the workers.[58] They should take part in formulating the new government's economic policy fully aware of their enormous weight in society. But they should handle the double-edged weapon of a strike gin-

[58]I do not want to advise the trade unions against actively participating in the shaping of national economic policy. But I do want to emphasize that the microlevel tasks ahead are fairly large: these tasks include local safeguarding of employees' interests, fighting for better work conditions, presenting a united front against those local managers who are prone to abuse their power, and the elimination of internal tensions within firms. Probably much more could be done in this area than what has been achieved so far. Meanwhile, there are other issues that require safeguarding the interests of *entire professions,* and which call for the active participation of the unions. But in the given situation all these tasks cannot be reduced to one single target, namely the raising of redistributive claims and demands for wage increases for their respective professions larger than those obtained by others. Should all the professions do this, it would lead to the very situation I have warned against: wage discipline would slacken and the wage-price spiral would start up again.

gerly. After all, the country's economic recovery depends first on whether the main actors in the economy can agree with one another, and then on whether they can abide by that agreement.

(b) *Unemployment.* The threat of unemployment has been mentioned earlier. At the risk of some repetition, it must be mentioned again here among the sources of tension.

The following demand has been voiced: jobs may only be abolished if new jobs have been found for all the workers *beforehand.* In my view there is no guaranteeing the fulfillment of that demand. It would be irresponsible for any government to promise to do so. The demand cannot be advanced by a union movement seeking to take part constructively in the country's recovery.

It cannot even be ensured in a consolidated market economy. The faster and more flexibly production adapts to the prevailing market conditions, the more common it is for jobs in one place or another to be eliminated. A fast and flexible adaptation of production such as this is expedient.

Fulfillment of this demand for job rights would be particularly absurd in the midst of the serious operation outlined in chapter 2. The message there is precisely that we neither can nor want to decide "structural policy" from behind a desk, but that we entrust the mutual adjustment of supply and demand to the market. There is no way of working out market prices in advance, and consequently no way of telling which factory will make permanent losses. It must be frankly admitted that this operation will cause a great shock. So how can we guarantee that for

197

each and every employee whose job is lost in the midst of the upheaval there will be another factory waiting with open arms, with another machine or desk inside it, and another apartment for him as well?

Instead of promises that cannot be kept, there are some realistic commitments that can be made. This study makes a distinction between transitional measures and the establishment of a lasting, long-term relationship between the labor market and job rights.

As far as the transitional measures are concerned, p. 163 already mentioned the "humanitarian" reserves for the period of the operation. Aid must be given to all whom the stabilization lands in trouble until they are able to adapt to the new situation. I do not see it as my task in this study to work out what form that aid should take or what conditions should be attached to it. The comment I do attach applies not to the size or means of dispensing the assistance but to its spirit. This is not a humiliating handout; it is a manifestation of society's solidarity with those who have been subjected to a grave trauma through no fault of their own. There must be human respect for the dignity of people in need of this assistance during these difficult months.

Returning to the longer term, we must learn to live with the idea that there will *always* be frictional unemployment. (We should note, incidentally, that there has always been frictional unemployment in all, including socialist, economies, but we knew little about its scale.) The more adaptable an economy is, the more common it is for jobs, or even whole firms or industries, to disappear. To use the great Austrian-born economist Schumpeter's famous expression, the condition for development is *creative destruction,* and where there is destruction, there are job losses. So we must construct a system of institutions and legal regulations related to frictional unemployment, ranging from unemployment benefits to retraining schemes to housing mobility and the chance to move from one place to another. This is one area in which there is a great need for cooperation between the government and the trade unions.

Finally, the most important safeguard against lasting mass unemployment is economic growth. In fact, to put it even more strongly: it is the *only* safeguard. One of the greatest achievements of the socialist planned economy in Hungary and many other socialist countries was full employment. This was achieved not by incorporating the right to work in its constitution but by a specific strategy of economic growth. But the way to preserve this achievement of the earlier economic system is not through a struggle in which strikes, threats, and political pressure are used to insist on an "acquired right" to full employment. The object must be for the economy to take off again, so that growth can create more and more jobs.[59]

While we alarm one another with the specter of unem-

[59]Within the framework of a socialist economic system, the absorption of excess labor is ensured primarily by a specific growth strategy, known as *forced growth.* The drawbacks of this strategy are numerous: resources are wasted, distortions are created in the structure of the economy, and so on.

As was stressed above, we expect economic growth to create new jobs. However, we hope that now this will be accomplished by a *harmonic* growth strategy, clear of the countless drawbacks and distortions of forced growth.

Here I wanted only to refer to the theoretical aspects of the problem of growth; considerations of space do not allow me to go into details.

ployment, sometimes for good reason and sometimes to excess, there are numerous branches of the economy that suffer from labor shortage. This will be so to an even greater extent in the future. The service sector will have to grow much faster than hitherto, and it will require a great deal of labor. I would stress in particular the role of growth of the private sector. In the years ahead, because of its fast expansion, the private sector will be capable of absorbing an appreciable proportion of the labor released by the "big operation," provided that the bureaucratic obstacles to its development are removed.

(c) *The issue of the poor.* It would be fatal to the stabilization and the assurance of national economic prosperity if a scenario were to develop in which the government represented the economic points of view while the humanitarian points of view had to be represented *against it.* One could express this potentially damaging antagonism in another way. The government would stand up for the rich, and those who stood up for the poor would have to defy the government. Or there could be another dichotomy: the role of government would be technocratic, while the role of the opposition would be that of welfare policy advocate.[60]

I hope the reader senses that every line of this book is imbued with a concern for each individual human being. The basic objectives of the program are to enhance the material welfare of the general public. But I cannot evade the following problem: grave economic ills will make the

---

[60]Hungarian has adopted a term analogous to the German expression *Sozialpolitik* for what American and British authors tend to refer to as welfare policy.

position of the poorest citizens even more difficult. Therefore, I would like to make a few comments on welfare policy.

I would first like to reiterate that the most important measure for welfare policy these days is to curb inflation. Anyone who seriously thinks the poor need help should stand wholeheartedly by the stabilization program and refrain from all proposals that would undermine it.

My second comment is another reminder: a reserve must be set aside before the stabilization operation begins in order to provide assistance to those temporarily in difficulties.

Third, a welfare policy program covering several years is required. There are others far better qualified than I to express an opinion on its details. Let me take this opportunity to express my respect for those who, for many years, have championed the cause of the poor and disadvantaged passionately through practical deeds.[61] They are certainly prepared now to join many other experts in compiling such a program. For my part I would like to contribute in this book only to one or two economic and ethical sides of the question.

There is an inevitable clash during the formulation of a welfare policy program between two opposing points of view. The need is infinite, but the resources are finite. All welfare policymakers, all conscientious welfare policy officials, and all researchers and writers on social affairs could produce an unbroken catalogue of thousands of em-

[61]See the pioneering works of I. Kemény, and Zs. Ferge (1988, 1989) and O. Solt (1985).

bittering instances and case histories of poverty and suffering. Those with any sympathy for their fellow men cannot see or hear about these cases without being moved. On
the other side there is a country in desperate condition, up
to its eyes in debt. To an economist with a sense of social
responsibility, it is clear that only the effective growth of
production and an economic upswing can lead the country
out of this predicament. This will require investments; and
it assumes wages that give real incentives and, for that
matter, high earnings to those who provide the greatest
impetus with their enterprises. In addition, education and
scientific research must be improved in the interest of
long-term development. The list could go on.

In my view the only possibility is to set sensible upper
limits to welfare policy spending. It should not be necessary to have little daily battles, pitting the "welfare politicians" and "champions of the poor" against stone-hearted
"treasury men." After all, this is what a democratic Parliament and a responsible debate regarding the national
budget are for. Let each member of Parliament, bearing in
mind his own political responsibility, form an opinion regarding welfare spending. In reaching his decision, he
must take account of all other expenditure items, and of
the fact that spending must be covered from taxation.

Finally, a parliamentary decision, valid for one year,
might be reached. I think it would be more useful to decide this matter two or three years in advance, if possible,
so as to provide a framework for the planning work by
persons and institutions involved in elaborating the details
of welfare policy. The program they devise should be a
flexible one, indicating the tasks to be placed in reserve;

that is, those that can be carried out if the situation develops more favorably, as well as those to be omitted if the situation turns out to be worse than expected. Nevertheless, we must plan by and large how much Hungary today can afford to spend on welfare purposes. And that must be the starting point in thinking about welfare policy, not the magnitude of Swedish welfare payments. We can reconsider the share of welfare expenditures when the country's ills have been remedied and its per capita national income has reached Sweden's present level.

It is not without cause that I underline the role of *members of Parliament.* People identify with their functions in society. A minister of finance can be expected to emphasize the treasury's views when he addresses Parliament; that is his obligation. It is also desirable that the press should unearth the alarming cases of penury and suffering, and use them to influence public opinion and the consciences of members of Parliament. But ultimately a *decision must be made,* and to use the technical language of economists, the scarce resources must be allocated. The right and political responsibility to make that decision is that of Parliament and Parliament alone.

I would like to make yet another observation on the issue of the poor, again on a subject that has political, ethical, and economic aspects. I think a poor man's life will improve if his poverty lessens, not if other, previously prosperous people join him in his poverty. I know this is a debatable point of view, but I would like in any case to express my opinion emphatically. It is no kind of moral compensation to me if that part of the earnings, savings, or wealth of others that I might consider "too much" is taken away from them. For how much is too much? Let us say all is still right and proper if someone earns 50 percent more than I do. All right, let him earn twice as much. But five or six times as much? That is scandalously unjust.

Such a line of argument is indefensible. No one has the authority to stipulate what level of earnings or wealth is morally permissible, or to draw a line above which it becomes immoral. Once we start judging in that way, we are going straight down the road that leads to the confiscation of private property.

So I would propose that we refrain from comforting the poor members of Hungarian society by declaiming with resounding phrases against the "rich." Regardless of how many times the television news reports disapprovingly about people buying luxury goods or villas near Lake Balaton, the pensioner will not have more meat on his table. The pensioner must be given the meat. That is the real welfare policy, not egalitarian rhetoric.[62]

I would express myself in a less extreme way if this country had a long period of bourgeois development behind it, if sizable private property were already established, if we had the incentive that comes from the knowledge that private wealth amassed by honest toil and business integrity could be inherited by children and grandchildren. In other words, I would support a measure

[62]I would recall here a previous point made concerning the criteria of social justice. Social justice demands first and foremost a continuous improvement in the situation of the least well-off strata. This in turn necessitates incentives for better performance and for more entrepreneurship. And it is indispensable for this stimulation that the most efficient, the thriftiest, and the luckiest accumulate great wealth.

of redistributive taxation if I were a citizen of today's France, for instance, although as a citizen of the Western world, I would still find the extreme form of redistribution practiced in Sweden excessive. I would consider that even there it acts as a disincentive by inducing people to withhold performance and by impeding healthy accumulation. But as I am neither a Frenchman nor a Swede, I must address the problems of Hungary today.

Here I would like to emphasize what I said in chapter 1. We are only at the very beginning of the process of reembourgeoisement. The main item on the agenda is still to set the mind of every participant in the private sector at rest, reassuring the peasant smallholder, the farmer beginning to modernize, the private artisan, and the owner of a large private firm: "Have no fear, go ahead and accumulate!" The state must assure these people that it will not confiscate what is theirs, that it does not want to skim their "excessive" earnings at all costs, because it wants them to spend it voluntarily on investment. The state must convince them that it will neither deceive their heirs nor force them into various tricks to evade the laws of inheritance. It must be made clear that the state will no longer motivate them to spend all their wealth themselves, on the grounds that their children and grandchildren cannot inherit it anyway. The state must proclaim that it would rather see founders of dynasties than greedy, shortsighted adventurers, because the former will turn into the really solid entrepreneurs.

While we have apparently digressed from the subject of welfare policy, the foregoing is in fact crucial. All who shape public opinion and all who ultimately decide on the

205

nation's money matters in Parliament must understand that social demagoguery and egalitarian rhetoric are no substitute for tangible welfare policy *deeds* tailored to the real material burden that the budget can bear.

THE NEED FOR A STRONG GOVERNMENT

Only a strong government can implement the economic policy outlined in this study. This applies to the gradual changes presented mainly in chapter 1, and also to the major operation described in chapter 2. Many of the tasks ahead require strength and toughness. The government must quell, within its own ranks, the insolence that hinders the development of the private sector. It should firmly implement the fiscal and monetary policy Parliament lays down, and secure financial and wage discipline.

Of course, there are various kinds of "strong governments." A stabilization program accompanied by a great upheaval and a reinforcement of the market economy might be carried out by a repressive authoritarian administration, some military dictatorship of the Chilean or Turkish variety. One could advance strictly economic arguments against them: neither Pinochet nor the Chicago boys surrounding him after the coup would prosper in today's Hungarian economy with its vast state sector. But aside from the economic argument, I am not prepared to consider this variant for *political* and *ethical* reasons. Regardless of the economic results that might be accomplished by a government whose strength lies in repressive measures, I am strongly against paying such a price for stabilization.[63]

The other possibility is a government whose strength lies in the support of the people, one to which free elections have given a real popular mandate to set the economy right with a firm hand. Let me continue the image employed in chapter 2. One can perform an operation without even asking the patient's leave, just by anesthetizing him and doing what the doctor thinks should be done, but civilized societies do not condone such procedures. The doctor explains to the patient why the operation is necessary and what are the risks involved, and asks his permission to perform it. To my mind this and only this is the permissible course for the operation I recommend. The operation must be done, but the Hungarian people as the patient must give their consent through the voice of their elected representatives.

It is not the purpose of this study to guess the composition of the future Hungarian government—that is outside the scope of my field. I will confine myself to a single comment in this respect. The political, economic, and ethical conflicts discussed in this study are reflected also *within* each party and movement, for instance in the form of the factions and groups existing inside individual parties, or in the form of the not-infrequent self-contradic-

[63]The view has become prevalent that repressive, authoritarian systems are more efficient in accomplishing macroadjustment tasks and executing stabilizing measures. This is erroneous: the comparison of forty-four authoritarian and thirty-nine democratic systems showed that none of these systems were markedly better at solving these tasks than the others. See S. Haggard and R. R. Kaufman (1989), p. 63.

tions and inconsistencies in the programs of particular parties. One finds both an idea and its opposite advocated at once, or extremely grave conflicts glossed over. Yet in fact these conflicts exist, and an increase in economic difficulties will exacerbate them.

In common parlance and in political science, the notion of a coalition is used in two senses. The *narrower* meaning refers to certain parties or political forces combining in a *government*. The *broader* meaning denotes some form of cooperation between certain parties, movements, groups, and social forces to perform common tasks. (There was a coalition in the West Germany of Adenauer and Erhard between the Christian Democratic government, the private sector, and the trade union movement, which *refrained* from exercising its right to strike.) I use the term "coalition" in that broader sense, leaving open the question of which forces in the coalition, broadly understood, will play a direct part in the government, and which will stay outside the government but without obstructing it. The latter may act as a constructive opposition but not seek confrontation on the basic economic tasks.

As for the future Hungarian coalition (in the broader sense), it needs a truly enterprising private sector with faith in its own future. But this private sector must not be faced by a state bureaucracy that, fearful for its own position, places hurdles in its way at every opportunity. And the government's policy must not be opposed by industrial workers grinding their teeth, because they feel they are losing from the transformation and are incited to action by competing trade unions. The success of the economic transition depends on whether the conflicts that may arise between these forces can be bridged and peaceful agreement reached.[64]

This study has attempted to sum up the tasks on which I think the participants in the future coalition (in the narrower and broader sense) need to agree. If they succeed, and keep to their agreement, there is hope that the country's economy can be set right and development can be speeded up. If they fail, and the coalition falls apart, if it is attacked or smashed from the start or after a short initial grace period, the economy will continue to slide helplessly downhill.

[64]A noteworthy collection has been compiled of studies that discuss the *fragility* of coalitions supporting new democracies that replace authoritarian regimes (see J. M. Nelson [1989]). These studies are based on Latin American, African, and Asian experiences. In many respects the situation is different in Eastern Europe, but a parallel can still be drawn, in that there is a need for agreement among some basic social groups in order to stabilize the new democracies politically and economically.

4

A Personal Postscript

ALTHOUGH I have written this study in the first person, out of personal conviction, I have tried throughout to keep to the subject. Having reached the end of what I have to say, I wish to add a few personal notes. There is a wave of biography breaking over Hungary, and I would rather refrain from contributing to it, but I cannot avoid mixing one or two biographical details into these final notes.

In the summer of 1956, as a young staff member of the Hungarian Academy of Sciences' Institute of Economics, I headed a small working group that elaborated a proposal for reforming the Hungarian economy. In many ways the material of the 150 or so pages compiled at that time anticipated the ideas that materialized later in the 1968 reform. In retrospect, I consider that proposal naive. Even if it had been applied in its entirety, it certainly would not have solved any of the basic systemic problems.

Thirty-three years have gone by in which I have never once undertaken to draw up another comprehensive economic policy proposal. Some of my work has yielded certain conclusions on economic policy, and I have occasionally made partial proposals, but I have never written a comprehensive program.

I have considered it my calling in the last few decades to study the socialist economy ("existing socialism," as it was referred to in socialist circles in and outside socialist countries), and to try to understand and explain how it works. I have seen myself as an observer and analyst of a living reality. In writing this pamphlet I have stepped only briefly out of the self-assigned role I will continue to consider my vocation. I have changed roles in this one study because this is a unique historic opportunity to do so. After many decades it seems for the first time that there will be a Parliament and a government before which I can place my ideas with confidence. What is more, this future Parliament and government will start work amid dreadful difficulties. So if some proposals have formed in my mind, this is the moment when I must present them.

I tried to write the study very quickly, although that is no excuse, of course, for any errors it may contain. In any case I refrained on this occasion from the repeated textual revisions permitted in more leisurely research. But although the text has been written quickly, the thoughts themselves are not improvised. I have been pondering these questions for many years, and the ideas follow closely from the research I have done over the decades. They arise from my studies of the socialist economic system and my attempt to compare that system in many contexts with past and present capitalist economies. This little book is an "economic policy pamphlet," but it comes from an author who has spent the last few decades and expects to concentrate his future energies on scientific research.

When engaged in my earlier (and future) field of activity—in descriptive-explanatory, theoretical works, what is called positive science—I must always ask myself what *predictive power* my propositions have. If such and such has happened up to now, what can be expected in the future? This question haunts me now, almost like a reflex, and I ask myself the question: Will all that this study proposes come to pass? And, of course, the same question was asked by those I have talked to about these problems.

I do not know. I have no illusions. I know the tremendous forces working against the realization of the ideas put forward; I know what perils lie in wait for the frail coalition needed for the realization of these proposals. But still, the proposal has a chance. I would like to hope that we do not miss that chance.

References

Alchian, Armen A. and Demsetz, Harold. 1973. "The Property Rights Paradigm." *Journal of Economic History* 33, no. 17 (March).

Antal, László. 1979. "Development—with Some Digression: The Hungarian Economic Mechanism in the Seventies." *Acta Oeconomica* 23, nos. 3–4: 257–273.

Antal, László. 1985. *Gazdaságirányítási és pénzügyi rendszerünk a reform útján* (The Hungarian System of Economic Control and Finance in the Process of Reform). Budapest: Közgazdasági és Jogi Könyvkiadó.

Barone, Enrico. 1908. "The Ministry of Production in the Collectivist State." In F. A. Hayek (1935), pp. 245–290.

Bársony, Jenő. 1989. "Hol tart a tulajdonreform ügye?" (Whither the Ownership Reform?) *Közgazdasági Szemle* 36, no. 5: 585–596.

Bauer, Tamás. 1976. "The Contradictory Position of the Enterprise under the New Hungarian Economic Mechanism." *Eastern European Economics* 15, no. 1 (Fall): 3–23.

Békesi, László. 1989. "Jövedelmi reform—elosztási igéretek nélkül" (Reform of Incomes—without Promise of Distribution). Conversation between Iván Wiesel and László Békesi. *Társadalmi Szemle* 44, no. 7: 16–23.

Belyó, Pál and Dexler, Béla. 1985. *Nem szervezett (elsősorban illegális) keretek között végzett szolgáltatások* (Services Supplied within a Non-Organized, Mainly Illegal Framework). Manuscript. Budapest: Szolgáltatáskutatási Intézet, KSH.

Bergson, Abram. 1948. "Socialist Economics." In H. S. Ellis (ed.), *A Survey of Contemporary Economics.* Homewood, Ill.: Irwin, pp. 1412–1448.

213

References

Brus, Wlodzimierz. 1972. *The Market in the Socialist Economy.* London: Routledge and Kegan Paul.

Consultative Committee for Economic Management. 1988. "A szocialista piacgazdaság megteremtése: Tézisek a gazdasági reformkoncepciót kidolgozó munkabizottságok számára" (Creation of the Socialist Market Economy: Theses for the Committees Working Out the Concept of Economic Reform). *Figyelő* (December 8), pp. 1 and 17–20.

Csoór, Klára and Mohácsi, Piroska. 1985. "Az infláció tényezői, 1980–1984" (The Main Factors of Inflation, 1980–1984). *Gazdaság* 19, no. 2: 21–39.

Demsetz, Harold. 1967. "Toward a Theory of Property Rights." *American Economic Review* 57, no. 2 (May): 347–359.

Domar, Evsey D. 1987. *The Blind Men and the Elephant: An Essay on Isms.* Mimeographed. Cambridge, Mass.: MIT (Department of Economics, Working Paper no. 473).

Erdős, Tibor. 1989. "Átgondolt gazdaságpolitikát! A külső és a belső egyensúly, a gazdasági növekedés és az infláció problémái" (A Well-Considered Economic Policy: The Problems of External and Internal Equilibrium, Economic Growth, and Inflation). *Közgazdasági Szemle* 36, no. 6: 545–557.

Ferge, Zsuzsa. 1988. "Gazdasági és szociális érdekek és politikák" (Economic and Social Interests and Policies). *Gazdaság* 12, no. 1: 47–64.

Ferge, Zsuzsa. 1989. "A negyedik út" (The Fourth Way). *Valóság* 32, no. 4: 7–19.

Fisher, Irwing. 1942. *Constructive Income Taxation.* New York: Harper.

Furubotn, Erik G. and Pejovich, Svetozar (eds.). 1974. *The Economics of Property Rights.* Cambridge, Mass.: Ballinger.

Gábor, István R. 1979. "The Second (Secondary) Economy: Earning Activity and Regrouping of Income outside the Socially Organized Production and Distribution." *Acta Oeconomica* 22, nos. 3–4: 291–311.

Gábor, István R. 1988. "Lépéskényszerek és kényszerlépések: Jegyzetek két évtized kormányzati munkaerő- és bérpolitikájáról" (Being Forced to Take Steps and the Forced Steps: Notes on Governmental Labor and Wage Policy over Two Decades). *Közgazdasági Szemle* 35, nos. 7–8: 803–807.

Gábor, István R. and Galasi, Péter. 1981. *A "második" gazdaság: Tények és hipotézisek* (The "Second" Economy: Facts and Hypotheses). Budapest: Közgazdasági és Jogi Könyvkiadó.

Gábor, István R. and Kővári, György. 1987. "A munkaerőpiac állami koordinációja és a bérszabályozás" (The State Coordination of the Labor Market and the Wage Regulation). *Gazdaság* 21, no. 4: 48–58.

Haggard, Stephan and Kaufman, Robert R. 1989. "Economic Adjustment in New Democracies." In J. M. Nelson (1989), pp. 57–78.

Hankiss, Elemér. 1989. *Kelet-európai alternatívák* (Eastern European Alternatives). Budapest: Közgazdasági és Jogi Könyvkiadó.

Hayek, Friedrich A. (ed.). 1935. *Collectivist Economic Planning.* London: Routledge and Kegan Paul.

References

Hayek, Friedrich A. 1944. *The Road to Serfdom*. Chicago: University of Chicago Press.

Juhász, Pál. 1981. "Társadalmi csoportok együttmüködése az első, második és harmadik ökonomiában" (Cooperation of Social Groups in the First, Second, and Third Economies). *Fogyasztói Szolgáltatások*, no. 4.

Kidric, Boris. 1985. *Sabrana dela*. Beograd: Izdavacki Centar Komunist.

Kis, János. 1986. *Vannak-e emberi jogaink?* (Do We Have Human Rights?) Budapest: Független Kiadó.

Kolodko, Grzegorz W. and McMahon, Walter W. 1987. "Stagflation and Shortageflation: A Comparative Approach." *Kyklos* 40, no. 2: 176–197.

Kornai, János: 1959. *Overcentralization in Economic Administration*. London: Oxford University Press.

Kornai, János. 1990. *Vision and Reality, Market and State: New Studies on the Socialist Economy and Society*. Hemel Hempstead: Harvester-Wheatsheaf, and Budapest: Corvina (forthcoming).

Kornai, János and Matits, Ágnes. 1987. *A vállalatok nyereségének bürokratikus ujraelosztása* (The Bureaucratic Redistribution of Firms' Profit). Budapest: Közgazdasági és Jogi Könyvkiadó.

Kovács, János Mátyás. 1990. "Reform Economics: The Classification Gap." *Daedalus* 119, no. 1 (Winter): 215–248.

Laki, Mihály. 1989. *Alternatívák és az alternatívok: Az uj politikai szervezetek gazdasági nézetei* (Alternatives and the Alternatives: The Economic Ideas of the New Political Organizations). Manuscript. Budapest: Közgazdasági Információs Szolgálat, August 4.

Lange, Oscar. 1936–37. "On the Economic Theory of Socialism." *Review of Economic Studies* 4, nos. 1–2 (October 1936 and February 1937): 53–71 and 123–142.

Lavoie, Don. 1985. *Rivalry and Central Planning: The Socialist Calculation Debate Reconsidered*. Cambridge: Cambridge University Press.

Lengyel, László. 1989. *Végkifejlet* (Denouement). Budapest: Közgazdasági és Jogi Könyvkiadó.

Liberman, Evsey G. 1972. "The Plan: Profit and Bonuses." In A. Nove and D. M. Nuti (eds.), *Socialist Economics: Selected Readings*, pp. 309–318. Middlesex: Penguin Books.

Mises, Ludwig von. 1920. "Economic Calculation in the Socialist Commonwealth." In F. A. Hayek (1935), pp. 87–130.

Musgrave, Richard A. and Musgrave, Peggy B. 1980. *Public Finance in Theory and Practice*. New York: McGraw-Hill.

Nelson, Joan M. (ed.). 1989. *Fragile Coalitions: The Politics of Economic Adjustment*. New Brunswick and Oxford: Transaction Books.

Niskanen, William A. 1971. *Bureaucracy and Representative Government*. Chicago: Aldine.

Nozick, Robert. 1974. *Anarchy, State, and Utopia*. New York: Basic Books.

Péter, György. 1954a. "A gazdaságosság jelentőségéről és szerepéről a népgaz-

215

References

daság tervszerü irányításában" (On the Importance and Role of Economic Efficiency in the Planned Control of National Economy). *Közgazdasági Szemle* 1, no. 3: 300–324.

Péter, György. 1954b. "Az egyszemélyi felelős vezetésről" (On Management Based on One-Man Responsibility). *Társadalmi Szemle* 9, nos. 8–9: 109–124.

Péter, György. 1956. "A gazdaságosság és jövedelmezőség szerepe a tervgazdaságban I–II" (The Role of Economic Efficiency and Profitability in the Planned Economy I–II). *Közgazdasági Szemle* 3, no. 6: 695–711, and nos. 7–8: 851–869.

Pető, Iván. 1989. "Polgárosodás, restauráció nélkül" (Embourgeoisement without Restoration). *2000* (August), pp. 5–8.

Petschnig, Mária Zita. 1986. "Inflációs feszültségek és megoldásaik" (Inflationary Tensions and Their Solutions). *Gazdaság* 20, no. 4: 38–51.

Rawls, John. 1971. *A Theory of Justice.* Cambridge: Harvard University Press.

Sachs, Jeffrey D. and Lipton, David. 1989a. *Exchange Rate Convertibility.* Mimeographed. Cambridge: Harvard University.

Sachs, Jeffrey D. and Lipton, David. 1989b. *Money and Credit Policy to Achieve Low Inflation.* Mimeographed. Cambridge: Harvard University.

Sárközy, Tamás. 1989. "Egy törvény védelmében I–II" (In Defense of a Law I–II). *Figyelő* (August 24 and 31), p. 3.

Schroeder, Gertrude E. 1988. "Property Rights Issues in Economic Reforms in Socialist Countries." *Studies in Comparative Communism* 21, no. 2 (Summer): 175–188.

Scitovsky, Tibor. *Welfare and Competition.* 1971. Homewood, Ill.: Irwin.

Sen, Amartya. "Freedom of Choice: Concept and Content." 1988. *European Economic Review* 32, nos. 2–3 (March): 269–294.

Solt, Ottília. 1985. "Szegények pedig nincsenek" (There Are No Poor). In G. Havas, J. Kenedi, and Gy. Kozák (eds.), *Isten éltessen Pista: Kemény István 60. születésnapjára* (God Bless You, Pista: On the 60th Birthday of István Kemény). Budapest: Samizdat.

Stiglitz, Joseph E. 1986. *Economics of the Public Sector.* 2nd ed. New York and London: W. W. Norton.

Storey, David J. (ed.) 1983. *The Small Firm: An International Survey.* London and Canberra: Croom Helm, and New York: St. Martin's Press.

Sun, Yefang. 1982. "Some Theoretical Issues in Theoretical Issues." In K. K. Fung (ed.), *Social Needs versus Economic Efficiency in China.* Armonk, N.Y.: M.E. Sharpe (works originally published between 1958 and 1961).

Széchenyi, István. 1979. *Hitel* (Credit). Budapest: Közgazdasági és Jogi Könyvkiadó.

Szelényi, Iván. 1986. *Szocialista polgárosodás* (Socialist Embourgeoisement). Manuscript. October.

Szelényi, Iván. 1988. *Socialist Entrepreneurs: Embourgeoisement in Rural Hun-*

gary. With the contribution of P. Manchin, P. Juhász, B. Magyar, and B. Martin. Madison: University of Wisconsin Press.

Tardos, Márton. 1980. "The Role of Money: Economic Relations between the State and the Enterprises in Hungary." *Acta Oeconomica* 25, nos. 1–2: 19–35.

Tardos, Márton. 1988a. "A gazdasági szervezetek és a tulajdon" (The Economic Organizations and the Question of Ownership). *Gazdaság* 22, no. 3: 7–21.

Tardos, Márton. 1988b. "A tulajdon" (The Question of Ownership). *Közgazdasági Szemle* 35, no. 12: 1405–1423.

Taylor, Fred M. 1929. "The Guidance of Production in a Socialist State." *American Economic Review* 19, no. 1: 1–80.

Tímár, János. 1985. *A társadalmi újratermelés időalapja* (The Total of Man-Hours Available for Social Reproduction). Manuscript. Budapest: Marx Károly Közgazdaságtudományi Egyetem.

Várhegyi, Éva. 1989. *Results and Failures of Monetary Restriction.* Mimeographed. Budapest: Pénzügykutató Rt.

Vissi, Ferenc. 1989. "Infláció a gazdaság stabilizálásának időszakában" (Inflation during the Stabilization of the Economy). *Gazdaság* 23, no. 1: 5–28.

Index

219

Index

Index

Tobin, James, 145n
trade:
  with Comecon countries, 165–66
  imports, 131–33, 158
trade union movement, 196–97

unemployment, 197–200
United States:
  congressional supervision of
    bureaucracy, 60–61
  budget deficit, 114–15
  impersonalization of property, 76–77

Várhegyi, E., 139n
Vissi, F., 106n

wage discipline:
  labor management and, 98–100
  macrodemand management and,
    142–45
  in state sector, 65, 77–80, 195

welfare policy, 200–201
  egalitarian values and, 203–6
  framework for, 202–3
  "humanitarian" reserve, 163–64, 165,
    198, 201
  inflation and, 109
  Parliament's responsibility for, 203
  spending limits, 202
Western economies as models for
    Eastern Europe, 20, 44–45n,
    52n, 190
  nonprivate ownership and, 75–77
West's interest in Eastern European
    developments, 18–19
Wiesel, I., 105n
World Bank, 11
World Institute for Development
    Economics Research (WIDER), 9

Yefang Sun, 57n
Yugoslavia, 99–100, 139, 143